MĀORI
TRIBES OF NEW ZEALAND

Te Ara – the Encyclopedia of New Zealand
www.TeAra.govt.nz

David Bateman

TE MANATŪ TAONGA
MINISTRY FOR CULTURE & HERITAGE

ABOUT TE ARA

Te Ara – The Encyclopedia of New Zealand is an online multimedia encyclopedia available free on the internet at **www.teara.govt.nz**. In Māori, 'te ara' means 'the pathway', and Te Ara offers many pathways to understanding New Zealand. It has been developed in themes by a team at the Ministry for Culture and Heritage – Te Manatū Taonga, and is a comprehensive guide to the country's peoples, natural environment, history, culture, economy and society.

Front cover, from left: Māori carving at Te Tii Marae, Waitangi, Focus New Zealand Photo Library Ltd; Mt Ngāuruhoe, Jakub Pavlinec/Shutterstock.
Back cover, from left: Te Tira Hōu perform at the 2003 Hui Ahurei at Rūātoki, Leanne Tamaki/Te Ara Encyclopedia of New Zealand; Martin Davis (right) of Ngā Rauru and Margaret Wilson, minister in charge of Treaty negotiations, hongi at the signing of the Ngā Rauru deed at Parliament, 2003, Office of Treaty Settlements; The Te Kawau Mārō o Maniopoto Festival, 2004, Hone Thompson/Private Collection.

Copyright © Crown copyright, 2008
Copyright © in typography and design David Bateman Ltd, 2008

Copyright in the illustrations not attributed to Te Ara – the Encyclopedia of New Zealand is held by the individual owners of the illustrations.

Published 2008 by David Bateman Ltd,
30 Tarndale Grove, Albany, Auckland, New Zealand

Reprinted 2010, 2013, 2014, 2015 (twice), 2016, 2017, 2018

ISBN: 978-1-86953-739-5

This book is copyright. Except for the purpose of fair review, no part may be stored or transmitted in any form or by any means, electronic or mechanical, including recording or storage in any information retrieval systems, without permission in writing from the publisher. No reproduction may be made, whether by photocopying or by any other means, unless a licence has been obtained from the publisher or its agent.

Design: Purrfect Grafix Ltd, Auckland
Printed in China through Colorcraft Limited, Hong Kong

CONTENTS

About Te Ara	2
Foreword	5
Pacific Migrations	6
Canoe Navigation	8
When Was New Zealand First Settled?	10
Ideas of Māori Origins	12
Hawaiki	14
Māori Creation Traditions	16
First Peoples in Māori Tradition	18
Canoe Traditions	20
Tribal Organisation	22
Muriwhenua tribes	24
Ngāpuhi	26
Whāngārei tribes	28
Ngāti Whātua	30
Tāmaki tribes	32
Hauraki tribes	34
Marutūahu tribes	36
Waikato	38
Ngāti Maniapoto	40
Te Arawa	42
Ngāti Tūwharetoa	44
Tauranga Moana tribes	46
Ngāti Awa	48
Te Whakatōhea	50
Ngāi Tūhoe	52
Te Whānau-ā-Apanui	54
Ngāti Porou	56
Tūranganui-a-Kiwa tribes	58
Ngāti Rongomaiwahine	60
Ngāti Kahungunu	62
Te Āti Awa of Taranaki	64
Taranaki	66
Ngāti Ruanui	68
Ngā Rauru Kītahi	70
Whanganui tribes	72
Ngāti Apa	74
Rangitāne	76
Muaūpoko	78
Ngāti Raukawa	80
Ngāti Toarangatira	82
Te Āti Awa of Wellington	84
Te Tau Ihu tribes	86
Ngāi Tahu	88
Moriori	90
Urban Māori	92
Glossary	94
Picture credits	95

Map of Iwi (Māori Tribes) of New Zealand

North Island:
- Muriwhenua tribes
- Ngāpuhi
- Whāngārei tribes
- Ngāti Whātua
- Tāmaki tribes
- Hauraki tribes
- Marutūahu tribes
- Tauranga Moana tribes
- Waikato
- Ngāti Awa
- Te Whakatōhea
- Te Whānau-ā-Apanui
- Ngāti Maniapoto
- Te Arawa
- Ngāti Porou
- Ngāi Tūhoe
- Ngāti Tūwharetoa
- Tūranganui-a-Kiwa tribes
- Ngāti Rongomaiwahine
- Te Āti Awa (Taranaki)
- Taranaki
- Ngāti Ruanui
- Ngā Rauru Kītahi
- Ngāti Kahungunu
- Whanganui tribes
- Ngāti Apa
- Rangitāne
- Muaūpoko
- Ngāti Raukawa
- Ngāti Toarangatira
- Te Āti Awa (Wellington)

South Island:
- Te Tau Ihu tribes
- Ngāi Tahu

Chatham Is.:
- Moriori

FOREWORD

The stories in this book concern the identity of Māori, the tangata whenua or people of this land. The first stories tell of how the Polynesian ancestors of Māori crossed the oceans in one of the great journeys of human history. The second part introduces the iwi (tribes) themselves, telling of their founding ancestors, their later history, their distinctive traditions and their life today. The list of tribes is not definitive. A number of smaller iwi do not have separate stories. However, all the major tribes of the country will be found here.

These stories began life as part of Te Ara, the online Encyclopedia of New Zealand. The first theme of Te Ara, launched in February 2005, included 45 entries on Māori New Zealanders, which were subsequently published in a book, *Māori peoples of New Zealand: Ngā iwi o Aotearoa*. The website also included a short story for each entry, a succinct and lively summary of the content. This book draws on these summaries to present a short introduction to the major tribes of New Zealand and the story of their arrival here.

Online these entries are published in both English and te reo Māori, alongside more than 1,200 maps, diagrams, photographs, sound files and moving images. A few of these images are reproduced here. To view all the multimedia resources and read the full entries, we encourage you to look at **www.TeAra.govt.nz**.

Many people have contributed to this book. The original essays on which this book is based were written by some very fine historians, many of whom came from the iwi they wrote about. The authors were: Tūhuatahi Tui Adams, Peter Adds, Te Awanuiārangi Black, Denise Davis, Mason Durie, Meihana Durie, Layne Harvey, Te Miringa Hōhaia, K. R. Howe, Grant Huwyler, Geoff Irwin, Taituha Kīngi, Morris Love, Rangi McGarvey, Paul Meredith, Hilary Mitchell, John Mitchell, Roka Paora, Mīria Pōmare, Darren Reid, Tamati Muturangi Reedy, Te Ahukaramū Charles Royal, Tony Sole, Māui Solomon, Rāwiri Taonui, Paul Tapsell, Te Maire Tau, Nick Tūpara, Ranginui Walker, Mere Whaanga, Carl Walrond, Martin Wikaira and David Young.

Extensive advice on the shape of the entries and the choice of authors came from Te Ara Wānanga, a committee of Māori scholars who oversee the Māori content of Te Ara. The members were: Ranginui Walker (chair), Peter Adds, Mason Durie, Edward Ellison, Ngapare Hopa, Keri Kaa, Wharehuia Milroy, Te Ahukaramū Charles Royal, Hone Sadler, Piri Sciascia, Monty Soutar, Mere Whaanga and Martin Wikaira.

The stories were edited by a team from the Ministry for Culture and Heritage – Te Manatū Taonga under the leadership of Jock Phillips (general editor) and Rangi McGarvey (Māori editor). A large team contributed to image research and editing. The material in this book, based on the original entries, was written by Tessa Copland and Fiona Oliver under the direction of Ross Somerville. The preparation of this book has been largely in the hands of Caren Wilton with advice from Basil Keane.

PACIFIC MIGRATIONS

The world's first seafarers set off from South-East Asia, sailing into the Pacific on simple rafts. Thousands of years later their Polynesian descendants began exploring further east, guided by the stars and the winds.

How did they survive these journeys into the unknown? And when did they discover New Zealand, the final major land mass? Radiocarbon dating and computer voyaging have provided a wealth of insights.

It is believed that the original ancestors of Polynesians originated in the area around Taiwan and then moved south and east. They mixed with other Melanesian peoples already living in Near Oceania, and over time the culture known as Lapita developed. Lapita people eventually settled Fiji, Samoa and Tonga, where the Polynesian culture emerged. During the first millennium AD Polynesians sailed east into French Polynesia and the Marquesas, and then migrated to Hawaii (600 AD) and Easter Island (700 AD). New Zealand was the last major land mass to be settled, around 1250–1300 AD.

The Pacific was the first ocean to be explored. But New Zealand's isolated islands, in the cold south-western waters of this ocean, were the last to be settled. Migration eastwards across the vast expanse of water occurred over thousands of years.

ANCIENT VOYAGING
From 50,000 to 25,000 BC people from Asia sailed simple rafts from island to island, reaching Near Oceania (Australia, New Guinea and the Solomon Islands). They traded in stone, hunted animals and gathered seafood and local plants.

RECENT VOYAGING
From 1200 BC seafarers sailed canoes further east, into Remote Oceania (Melanesia, Micronesia and Polynesia). The islands were much further apart and more difficult to find. Migrating voyagers kept in contact with their home islands through trading trips.

THE LAPITA PEOPLE

The Lapita were the first to reach Remote Oceania. Between 1200 and 1000 BC they spread to West Polynesia (including Tonga and Samoa). On single-hulled outrigger canoes they brought pigs, dogs, chickens, yams and bananas; they also invented a new style of pottery, decorated with faces.

A human face stares from these remnants of Lapita pottery, dated to 1000 BC.

POLYNESIAN EXPLORERS

About 3,000 years ago Polynesian culture developed in West Polynesia. Skilled navigators in double-hulled canoes gradually discovered remote islands to the east, using their knowledge of the stars and the winds to return home safely. Groups would then set off to start new settlements. Migration through East Polynesia began after 1 AD. By 1000 AD they had reached South America, and returned.

REACHING NEW ZEALAND

Using small islands as stepping-stones, explorers finally discovered New Zealand. Archaeologists believe that the first settlers came no later than 1300 AD. (There is tentative evidence of Pacific rats arriving 1,200 years earlier – but if so, the people who brought them died out or moved on.)

The original migrants came from a region in East Polynesia which Māori later called Hawaiki. Bringing dogs and rats, taro and kūmara (sweet potato) to New Zealand, they found plenty of wildlife, including birds now extinct: the moa, a species of swan, and the giant Haast's eagle.

Excavated from an archaeological site in New Zealand in 1964, this fishing lure shank was made from a tropical pearl oyster shell. It is one of very few such items that archaeologists are certain came from Polynesia.

The Solomon Islands, some of which are shown here, lie at the eastern edge of Near Oceania. It seems that early seafarers knew how to cross from island to island, even where islands were not visible to each other. It is unlikely that people had got from Asia as far east as the Solomon Islands by accidental drift voyages.

Māori Tribes of New Zealand

CANOE NAVIGATION

Thousands of years ago, the ancestors of Māori journeyed out of South-East Asia and into the Pacific. They sailed in waka (canoes), and were some of the world's greatest canoe builders, navigators and mariners.

Recently, replica canoes have been made as part of a renaissance of traditional culture. Although today's crafts rely on modern radio and navigation equipment for safety reasons, the spirit and relevance of traditional seafaring remains.

The earliest sailing vessels of Polynesian ancestors were rafts and dugout canoes. They were used on short voyages, but because dugouts capsized easily, and rafts were prone to swamping, they were not suitable for long distances.

Eventually, an outrigger (a second hull) was fixed to the side. This made canoes faster and more stable. With these changes people could sail across long stretches of open sea. Sails and steering paddles were added for greater speed and control.

Polynesian double-hulled canoes or twin-hulled canoes were similar to outrigger canoes. They were fast and easy to manoeuvre, and could sail rougher waters. They ranged in length from 20 metres for long trips, up to a giant 36 metres for shorter journeys. For comparison, Captain James Cook's ship, the *Endeavour*, was 33 metres long.

This carving on the threshold of a meeting house depicts a tipua (ancestral or spiritual creature). Similar carvings are found in many East Coast meeting houses. This creature is taken from the story of Uenuku and his sons Paikea and Ruatapu. Paikea is said to have survived a disaster in which many others were drowned. He was saved by whales — his tīpuna (ancestors), or tipua.

OCEAN VOYAGING

To prepare for the voyage, sailors stocked canoes with food and water. People would memorise the routes, or record them in songs. Directions were taken from the landscape in relation to the paths of stars.

Traditional navigators used the rising and setting points of stars and planets as signposts. During the day, the sun was a guide, and in overcast weather, ocean swells and wind direction were used to chart the way.

Ocean-going canoes have been built as part of the renaissance in Polynesian voyaging. Te Aurere (right), pictured here with Te Au-o-Tonga, was built by Hector Busby in 1991.

LOCATING LAND

Voyagers knew land was ahead even before they could see it. Migrating birds may have helped show the way to new lands, and fishing birds such as gannets, terns and petrels were a sign that land was not far away. Pods of whales may also have guided canoes to New Zealand – the ancestor Paikea is said to have arrived on a whale.

Navigators could also find land by reading the position of stars, the colour and formation of clouds, and the pattern of waves.

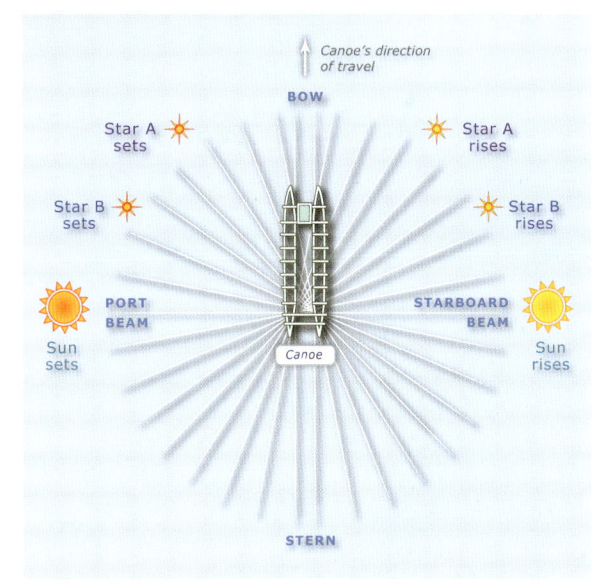

DECLINE AND REVIVAL OF CANOE VOYAGING

Once Europeans colonised the Pacific, knowledge of traditional navigation methods was lost. Canoes were replaced with ships. Eventually, some people came to believe that long-distance Pacific voyages were impossible.

Partly as a response to this, replica canoes were built and sailed. The *Hōkūle'a* was one of the first of these. In 1976 it completed a voyage from Hawaii to Tahiti and back.

The success of the *Hōkūle'a* inspired others to re-create ancient canoes and journeys. The *Hawaiki-nui*, perhaps the most authentic of these modern craft, sailed unharmed through dramatic storms.

This diagram shows a canoe, looking from above. The 360° horizon around the canoe was divided up into different sectors named 'houses' and these were marked on canoe railings. This canoe is travelling due north at the spring equinox, when the sun rises due east and sets due west. At night the rising and setting of stars were used to align the canoe in a direction of travel. For example, when Star A set, Star B was used, and so on through the night until the earth's own star, the sun, rose.

Paddles like this one (right) were used to propel small canoes throughout the Pacific. Paddles were also used to steer the craft as the canoes had no rudders. In smaller outriggers this was done by the person at the rear of the craft inserting their paddle into the water. In bigger ocean-going canoes a larger, specially designed paddle was used for steering.

Māori Tribes of New Zealand 9

WHEN WAS NEW ZEALAND FIRST SETTLED?

In 2570 BC the great pyramid of Giza in Egypt was completed. But the remote islands of New Zealand lay empty of human history. From 1200 BC the Lapita people spread to West Polynesia. In Europe, Roman civilisation rose and fell. By 700 AD the Arab empire was expanding, and in 1066 the Normans conquered Britain.

Still New Zealand remained unseen and unknown. Most evidence suggests that it was another two centuries before explorers from East Polynesia finally set eyes on the land at the end of the world. But was it really as late as that? Debate continues as to when the first footprint appeared on a New Zealand beach.

MIGRATING FROM AFRICA

The first humans evolved in Africa and left that continent about 100,000 years ago. They began to migrate and slowly settled most of the rest of the world. The islands of the Pacific, including New Zealand, were among the last places to be reached. It was only 3,200 years ago that people began heading eastward from Asia into the Pacific Ocean. They had great skill and courage to sail across vast stretches of open sea.

SIGNS OF SETTLEMENT

On the islands they settled, people left traces of where they had lit fires, killed animals, and brought in new animals such as rats. By studying these remains, archaeologists are able to estimate when the first settlers arrived. One of the main methods they use is radiocarbon dating, which measures the age of bones and wood.

There is a lot of evidence that Polynesian people first arrived in New Zealand around 1250–1300 AD, coming from East Polynesia in canoes.

These ash layers deposited by the eruptions at Taupō (232 AD ± 15) and Kaharoa (1314 AD ± 12) are exposed in peat at Waihī Beach, western Bay of Plenty. The Taupō ash layer can be seen just above the water level, and the Kaharoa ash layer is the light band in the middle. No direct archaeological evidence of human settlement has ever been found beneath either of these ash layers.

This huge sandstone slab, on the south Wairarapa coast, is named Ngā Rā o Kupe (Kupe's Sails), as it resembles the sail of a Polynesian double-hulled canoe. Kupe is an early ancestor of many Māori tribes, and is said to have camped on the flats near this rock as he explored the coastline. Some oral traditions place Kupe in genealogies around 21 generations ago, or in the late 1400s, well after the accepted date of Polynesian settlement of 1250–1300. While genealogies are a rich and fascinating resource, they do not provide an exact date for human settlement.

THE RAT BONES DEBATE

In the 1990s some rat bones were radiocarbon dated to much earlier, around 50–150 AD. As rats are not native to New Zealand and can't swim great distances, it was believed that they must have come with people, in canoes. So this new evidence raised the possibility that people, too, arrived at that time, but did not stay or leave any further signs. There is debate as to whether this much earlier date is accurate.

Did the first man or woman step onto a New Zealand beach around 1250–1300? Or, intriguingly, were there footprints in the sand over 1,000 years earlier?

The Pacific rat (kiore) is not native to New Zealand and so could only have arrived with humans.

Early Polynesians used this site, known as Wairau Bar, as a moa-hunting camp. As the moa is now thought to have become extinct very quickly, possibly within 100–200 years of human settlement, those who hunted it must have been among the first generations of Polynesian arrivals.

Māori Tribes of New Zealand 11

IDEAS OF MĀORI ORIGINS

Are Māori descendants of the Greeks and Egyptians? Were they one of the Lost Tribes of Israel – or was India their homeland? And did they arrive in one great fleet of canoes?

From their earliest encounters with Māori, European scholars were fascinated by the origins of New Zealand's inhabitants. More recently, scientific research has revealed compelling evidence of a Polynesian origin for Māori.

This handsome 1833 profile of Natai, the bouffant hairstyle recalling Napoleon, is regarded by art historians as an outstanding example of the European concept of the 'noble savage'. In the romantic period, indigenous peoples who lived close to nature were seen as living a truer life than convention-bound Europeans.

When Europeans discovered New Zealand, they wondered about the origins of the Māori people. Captain James Cook noticed that Polynesians and Māori had similar appearances and cultures. He believed they had migrated from the islands of South-East Asia. It is still agreed that Māori are Polynesians whose ancestors lived in the Taiwan region.

Some early visitors, who studied items such as headdresses and carvings, thought Māori ancestors might be ancient Greeks or Egyptians. One artist painted a Māori as a Roman warrior. Christian missionaries suggested that Māori ancestors were Jewish, belonging to the Lost Tribes of Israel.

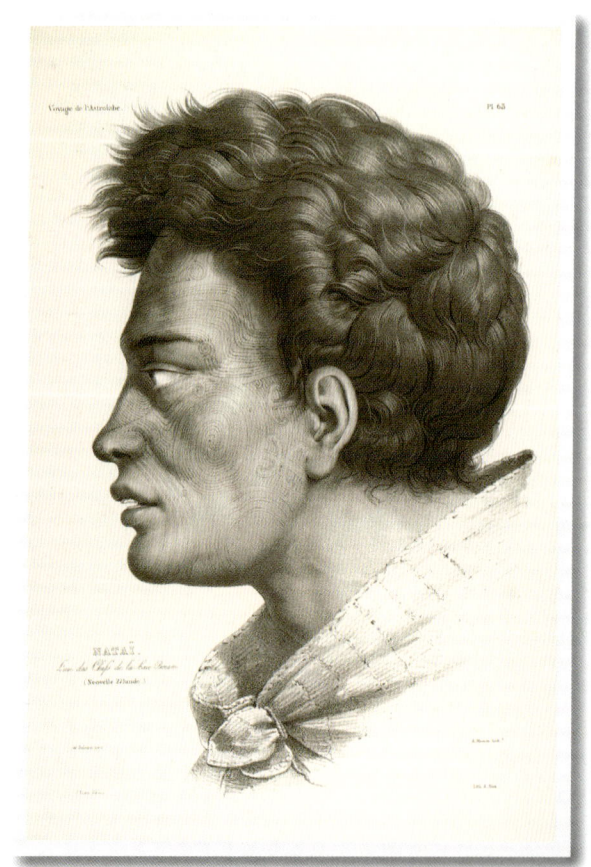

THE ARYAN THEORY

In the 1850s scholars discovered that most European languages had developed from Sanskrit, the ancient language of India. It is still believed that Europeans and Indians share ancestors, known as Aryan or Caucasian. Ethnologists such as Edward Tregear claimed that Māori, too, had come from India. He found similarities between Māori and Sanskrit words and symbols.

THE GREAT FLEET STORY

In the 19th century many scholars recorded different Māori stories about reaching New Zealand from Polynesia. But one man, Percy Smith, calculated from listening to Māori histories that they had migrated together in 1350 AD, in one 'great fleet' of seven canoes. According to Smith, they had then conquered the Moriori, who he said were a primitive Melanesian race already living in New Zealand. Smith's story was accepted for over 60 years. It was popular because many believed that European settlers were the next 'superior' people, who would take over from Māori.

12   Māori Tribes of New Zealand

In the late 1800s and early 1900s various theories had Māori originating in South America, North America, India, Greece, Egypt and Israel, among other places. This map shows the actual origin of the Māori people's Polynesian ancestors — around Taiwan. The arrows show their migration through South-East Asia, Melanesia and into the Pacific.

NEW UNDERSTANDING

From the 1920s scientists proved that Chatham Island Moriori, like Māori, were descendants of the original Polynesian settlers of New Zealand. Moriori had migrated to the Chatham Islands some time after 1300 AD, possibly around 1500.

In the 1960s errors were found in Percy Smith's research for the Great Fleet story. Recent scientific evidence includes DNA analysis, and radiocarbon dating of archaeological sites. It is now believed that Māori arrived at different times, from several points in East Polynesia, in the late 13th century.

Hawaiki – the homeland

Māori told early Europeans that their ancestors had sailed to New Zealand from Hawaiki, which is the name of their ancestral home. Some Māori placed it somewhere to the north-east of New Zealand.

Today it is believed that the most likely region from which Polynesians came to New Zealand is the Southern Cooks and Society Islands.

This romantic oil painting by Kennett Watkins, 'The legend of the voyage to New Zealand' (1912), shows a fleet of double-hulled, ocean-going canoes hauling ashore in New Zealand. Images such as this helped to popularise the myth of a Great Fleet for decades.

Māori Tribes of New Zealand

HAWAIKI

Hawaiki – a real island? Or a mythical place?
Hawaiki is the traditional Māori place of origin. The first Māori are said to have sailed to New Zealand from Hawaiki. And in Māori mythology Hawaiki is the place where Io, the supreme being, created the world and its first people. It is the place from which each person comes, and it is where each will return after death.

THE SOURCE OF LIFE

Hawaiki is a place of great importance in Māori tradition, and appears in many songs, proverbs and whakapapa (genealogies). In tradition, the ancestors of Māori came to New Zealand from Hawaiki, navigating the seas in their canoes.

Hawaiki is seen as the place from which humans are born, and to which they go after death – it is strongly associated with the cycle of birth, life and death. Hawaiki represents all that is good and powerful. It is a mystical place, where people turn into birds or descend to the underworld.

HOME OF THE GODS

In some traditions, the supreme being Io created Hawaiki. The gods are believed to live there, including the trickster demigod Māui, whose deeds are famous throughout Polynesia. The first woman, Hineahuone, was fashioned from the soil of Hawaiki.

LOCATION UNKNOWN

Māori and Pākehā alike have wondered about the true location of Hawaiki. The actual location has never been confirmed, and it is uncertain if it is a real, physical island, or a mythical place. Some have associated Hawaiki with the Tahitian island Ra'iātea (Rangiātea, in Māori). Like Hawaiki, Rangiātea is seen as both a physical and spiritual place.

Some people thought that Māori might have originated from Polynesia, India, or even Mesopotamia. More recent scholars admit it is difficult to decide on the 'true' location of a place that is also mythological.

Te Puna Wai Mātauranga (the wellspring of knowledge) was carved by Bob Koko and stands outside the University of Waikato library in Hamilton. It represents Tāwhaki, who was one of the supernatural inhabitants of Hawaiki. According to Tainui tradition he ascended the heavens and received the three baskets of knowledge.

Māui was one of the great characters of Hawaiki, renowned for his daring. This carving of Māui capturing the sun is from Te Hono ki Hawaiki at the Museum of New Zealand Te Papa Tongarewa.

Māori Tribes of New Zealand 15

MĀORI CREATION TRADITIONS

Every culture has its traditions about how the world was created. Māori have many of them, but the most important stories are those that tell how darkness became light, nothing became something, earth and sky were separated, and nature evolved.

Through the spoken repetition of these stories, the world is constantly being recreated.

The koru, often used in Māori art as a symbol of creation, is based on the shape of an unfurling fern frond (above).

Cliff Whiting's carving (top), 'Te wehenga o Rangi rāua ko Papa', depicts one version of the creation story, which tells how the god Tāne Mahuta raised the sky by standing on his head and pushing upwards with his feet.

Like all societies, Māori have traditions about how the world was created. Although various tribes tell different versions of the creation story, there are some themes in common. Most describe movement from Te Kore (nothingness) to something, and from Te Pō (darkness) to Te Ao (light).

The separation of earth and sky always features, as does talk of how the gods were responsible for making the natural world.

In the beginning Ranginui (the sky) and Papatūānuku (the earth) were joined together, and their children were born between them in darkness. The children decided to separate their parents, to allow light to come into the world. After this, the children became gods of various parts of the natural world. For example, Tāne became the god of the forests and Tangaroa the god of the sea.

VARIATIONS

Different tribes have their own variations of the creation story. In some of these, the god Tāne plays an important role in separating earth and sky. Others talk about a

16 Māori Tribes of New Zealand

supreme being, called Io. Not all tribes have an Io tradition, and Māori and Pākehā historians have debated whether Io is a pre-European or post-European concept.

CREATION AND RENEWAL

Often creation is summed up in lists, showing processes in the natural world. For example, the growth of a seed is described in a list that traces the movement from shoot to hair root. These whakapapa (genealogies) emphasise how life is constantly being recreated.

THE INFLUENCE OF CREATION TRADITIONS

Creation stories have influenced many aspects of the Māori view of the world. The gods who shaped the natural world, for instance, are seen as role models for human behaviour. And the repetition of stories and genealogies is seen as a creative act that mimics the original creation of the world.

This sculpture by Jason Porter (above), 'Te autahi ki te ākau' (one ocean current), is a modern representation of the god of the sea, Tangaroa, and his children. It stands at one of the entrances to Pāpāmoa Beach, Bay of Plenty.

Like all traditional Māori meeting houses, Te Tumu Herenga Waka at Victoria University of Wellington (right) contains the central images of creation. The roof represents Ranginui (the sky) and the floor Papatūānuku (the earth). The supporting posts represent those used by the god Tāne to separate earth and sky during the creation of the world.

Māori Tribes of New Zealand 17

FIRST PEOPLES IN MĀORI TRADITION

Among Māori tribes there are many oral traditions about ancient peoples and gods who inhabited New Zealand from the beginning of time.

From the gods of the natural world, to the mysterious people of the mountains, to the Polynesian explorer Kupe, stories of the ancestors have been handed down the generations. They are the bedrock of a deep connection with the land.

This poupou (carved column) is at Tāne-nui-a-rangi, the Waipapa marae at the University of Auckland. It shows Kupe holding a paddle — a token of his skill as a navigator — and the octopus of his enemy Muturangi.

LINKING THE PEOPLE TO THE LAND

Many Māori traditions tell of the Polynesian settlers from Hawaiki, who reached the coast in canoes about 700 years ago.

There are also myths and legends of earlier beings, such as the first human to be created. Through these stories, tribes can trace a long relationship with the land, and with the different regions they live in.

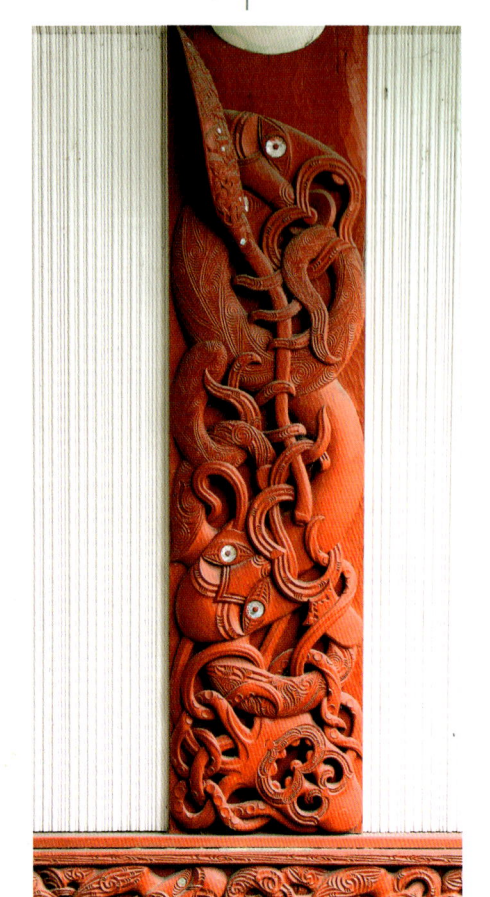

HINEAHUONE

In tradition, Ranginui (the sky father) and Papatūānuku (the earth mother) were the parents of Tāne. Tāne made the first woman from the soil, naming her Hineahuone.

One story says 'the arms, the body, the limbs, the thighs, these all took shape and the skeleton was complete'. With Tāne she had a daughter, Hinetītama, later known as Hine-nui-te-pō, who is seen in the dawn and in the setting sun. It is said that all human beings are descended from these ancestors.

MĀUI

The trickster demigod Māui is said to have dragged the North Island from the ocean, using the jawbone of his grandmother as a hook.

The Māori name for the island is Te Ika-a-Māui (Māui's fish). The many other stories about Māui tell of the theft of fire, the capture of the sun and the pursuit of immortality.

HINE-PŪKOHU-RANGI

Māori people believed that they were related to the natural world – the earth, the birds, the trees. The Ngāi Tūhoe tribe believe that their ancestor was Hine-pūkohu-rangi, the maiden of the mist that swirled around the Urewera mountains.

PATUPAIAREHE AND TŪREHU

There are many accounts of mysterious people who were already in New Zealand when Polynesian voyagers arrived by canoe. It is said that they lived high in the mountains, and could be heard calling to each other. Two of these groups were known as the patupaiarehe and the tūrehu.

KUPE

In many traditions, Kupe was the first Polynesian to discover New Zealand. He chased a great octopus across the ocean in his canoe, and finally killed it at Cook Strait. Kupe explored the country and named many places, such as Pari Whero (Red Rocks), on the Wellington coast.

TOITEHUATAHI

In some traditions the ancestor Toitehuatahi arrived from Hawaiki, and in others he was born in New Zealand. Tribes are proud to claim they are descended from Toi, and the Ngāti Awa people say his village overlooked the Bay of Plenty, near present-day Whakatāne.

While many Māori whakapapa (genealogies) trace ancestry back to arrivals from Hawaiki, some speak of origins directly from the land. Elsdon Best, the ethnographer, called the Tūhoe people 'children of the mist', because their genealogical tradition goes back to the mist-maiden Hine-pūkohu-rangi.

Toikairākau meeting house is at Waikirikiri marae, Rūātoki, in the northern Urewera, and is named after the early Polynesian settler Toi. Toi appears in many North Island tribal genealogies, often as the earliest ancestor living in New Zealand when many canoes arrive.

Māori Tribes of New Zealand

CANOE TRADITIONS

It was once believed that the ancestors of Māori came to New Zealand in a single 'great fleet' of seven canoes. We now know that many canoes made the perilous voyage from Polynesia.

Through stories passed down the generations, tribal groups trace their origins to the captains and crew of over 40 legendary vessels, from the *Kurahaupō* at North Cape to the *Uruao* in the South Island. Rich in conflict and drama, and blending history and symbolism, these canoe traditions form a founding narrative for Māori New Zealanders.

There are many Māori traditions about the arrival of ancestors in waka (canoes), from a place called Hawaiki in East Polynesia. Some people believed these accounts were literally true. Others have seen them as poetic imaginings. The reality is likely to be somewhere in between. These traditions contain information about distantly remembered voyages, but have been enriched over time.

CANOES OF THE NORTH
The major canoes of the northern people are:
- *Kurahaupō*, which landed near North Cape
- *Ngātokimatawhaorua* and *Māmari*, whose priests battled each other with powerful spells
- *Tinana* and *Te Māmaru*, important to the Te Rarawa and Ngāti Kahu tribes
- *Māhuhu-ki-te-rangi*, the most significant canoe for Ngāti Whātua people
- *Mataatua*, captained by Puhi, Miru and Te Wahineiti.

TAINUI AND TE ARAWA
There are many similarities between the *Tainui* and *Te Arawa* stories. Some people have suggested that the two canoes were actually the twin hulls of one

Takapaukura (Tom Bowling Bay), near North Cape, is where the Kurahaupō canoe, captained by Pōhurihanga, is said to have landed.

20 Māori Tribes of New Zealand

boat which separated on arrival in New Zealand. *Te Arawa* made final landfall at Maketū in the Bay of Plenty. The *Tainui* arrived at Kāwhia Harbour, between Auckland and New Plymouth.

MATAATUA

A major canoe of the Bay of Plenty area is the *Mataatua*, captained by Toroa. His sister (or in some stories, his daughter) bravely rescued the boat as it began to drift. From her cry, 'Me whakatāne au i ahau nei!' (I must act like a man!), the settlement of Whakatāne got its name.

EAST COAST STORIES

The East Coast has stories of the ancestor Paikea, who came to New Zealand on the back of a whale.

Two important canoes are the *Horouta*, which brought kūmara (sweet potato), and the *Tākitimu*, whose crew were the ancestors of Ngāti Kahungunu.

AOTEA

The *Aotea* canoe arrived near Kāwhia, but the crew then journeyed south before settling around Pātea, so named because that is where they threw down their burdens (pātea).

SOUTHERN CANOES

There are many canoe legends associated with the South Island. In one, the *Ārai-te-uru* was caught in a storm and its cargo of kūmara was washed ashore – they remain today as the massive Moeraki boulders.

In another, the captain Rākaihautū sailed the *Uruaokapuarangi* to present-day Nelson. He then explored the South Island, shaping the mountains and carving out lakes with his digging stick.

The *Tākitimu* canoe was wrecked at Te Waewae Bay, in the far south of the South Island.

Whakaotirangi, the wife of Ruaeo, was kidnapped by Tamatekapua and brought to New Zealand on the Te Arawa canoe. Both Tainui and Te Arawa traditions state that she was responsible for safeguarding the seed of the kūmara on the voyage. In this carving at Ōtāwhao marae, Te Awamutu, she holds a basket of kūmara.

The Tākitimu canoe is said to have explored the West Coast of the South Island. It was wrecked on the south coast, where it was transfixed as the Tākitimu Mountains, pictured below.

Māori Tribes of New Zealand

TRIBAL ORGANISATION

Generations ago, canoes sailed by Māori ancestors set out from East Polynesia and landed in New Zealand. From these founding peoples came the iwi (tribes) that form the structure of Māori society.

Within each iwi are many hapū (clans or descent groups), each of which is made up of one or more whānau (extended families). The bond that holds them together is one of kinship, both with a founding ancestor and with the many members of their iwi, hapū and whānau today.

WHAT ARE IWI AND HAPŪ?

The iwi (tribe) is the largest of the groups that form Māori society. Each iwi is made up of various hapū (clans or descent groups), which might have up to several hundred members. Traditionally, the main purposes of a hapū were to defend land, and to provide support for its members.

Some tribal groups formed from links to the waka (canoe) on which their founding ancestor arrived in New Zealand from Hawaiki. For example, the Waikato tribes trace their descent from the *Tainui* waka. Others developed when the pressure on resources such as land and food became so great that some members had to move away and establish themselves elsewhere. War, migration and family infighting also caused new iwi or hapū to emerge.

Iwi and hapū are often named after an ancestor. For example, Ngāpuhi means 'the people of Puhi' and Te Uri-o-Rātā means 'the descendants of Rātā'. Sometimes tribal names came from an important event that involved their ancestor, such as a battle.

Entitled 'Tu Kaitote, the pa of Te Wherowhero on the Waikato, Taupiri mountain in the distance', this lithograph is based on a watercolour painted by George French Angas in 1844. It shows how various buildings within the pā were grouped around a large central meeting place, with tall palisades around the perimeter.

The importance of older people within the whānau, especially their role in nurturing the young, is conveyed in this early 20th-century painting, 'The time of kai,' by Gottfried Lindauer. All generations, from elders to young children and babies, gather near the hāngī to partake of eel, kūmara and shellfish.

Each hapū was made up of different-ranking members, headed by chiefs called ariki and rangatira. First-born females also had high status. Experts in areas such as history and tradition, carving and healing were called tohunga. There were commoners, and sometimes slaves, in each hapū.

WHĀNAU – FAMILY

Each hapū is made up of whānau (extended families). Whānau included much-respected elders, adults, children and grandchildren. Everyone helped each other, working for the group and caring for each other's children and the elderly.

CHANGES AFTER EUROPEAN CONTACT

After New Zealand became a British colony, the way that iwi and hapū functioned began to change. When the government bought or confiscated Māori land in the 19th century, tribes were dispersed.

From the mid-20th century, when many younger people moved to the cities for greater work opportunities, tribal power was diminished. From the late 20th century, however, tribal organisations have worked to reconnect people with their tribal origins.

Nohorua, shown with his wife Te Wainokenoke and son Tuarau, was the half-brother of the Ngāti Toarangatira chief, Te Rauparaha. As the eldest in the whānau, Nohorua's rank was that of tuakana (senior). In addition he was trained as a tohunga, and was probably responsible for choosing the dates on which important initiatives were taken by Te Rauparaha and his followers.

Māori Tribes of New Zealand

MURIWHENUA TRIBES

Muriwhenua means 'this is the end of the land'. The Muriwhenua tribal territory forms the tail of Māui's fabled fish, including the northernmost tip of New Zealand – Cape Rēinga. Tradition holds that this is where spirits of the dead depart. Rich in such legends, the history of these six tribes is also one of ancestral lands lost and reclaimed.

The remarkable carving above, from about 1400 AD, was once thought to be a door lintel, but it is more likely a roof decoration, designed to be seen from both sides. Now in Auckland Museum, it originally came from Lake Tāngonge, near Kaitāia, in the heart of Te Rarawa territory.

The Muriwhenua people belong to six iwi (tribes):
- Ngāti Kurī
- Ngāi Takoto
- Te Pātū
- Ngāti Kahu
- Te Aupōuri
- Te Rarawa.

Muriwhenua territory is in the far north of New Zealand, extending from the Maungataniwha Range up to Cape Rēinga. It forms the tail of the fish that the legendary hero Māui pulled from the ocean – Te Ika-a-Māui, the North Island. Kupe, the great navigator, discovered this region after thinking he had seen a whale: in fact it was Houhora Mountain, north of Kaitāia.

Muriwhenua tribes have many traditions about the places named by the Polynesian navigator Kupe. His crew are said to have settled from Cape Rēinga (shown here) to Pārengarenga Harbour.

TRADITIONS

It is said that Ngāti Kurī, which means 'tribe of the dog', were named when they lured their enemy onto a beach by creating a whale out of dog skin.

Another tradition describes a clever escape from the besieged village of Murimotu. The chief Tūmatahina told his people to walk in a single line of footprints in the sand, so it looked as if only one person had left.

THE TREATY OF WAITANGI

In 1840, 61 Muriwhenua chiefs signed the Treaty of Waitangi, believing that it would protect their lands. But over the years the Muriwhenua people lost huge amounts of land to settlers or to the government.

From 1994, the tribes have lodged important claims with the Waitangi Tribunal, which are being settled with individual tribes.

The 1988 Muriwhenua fishing report was instrumental in the 1992 settlement of Māori claims to offshore fisheries.

MURIWHENUA TRIBES TODAY

In 2006, there were almost 40,000 Muriwhenua people. Many moved to the cities from 1950 onwards, and less than one-third remain in the ancestral homelands. Almost 17,000 live in the Auckland region.

There are several stories about the origins of Ngāti Kurī's name (kurī means dog). One says that they lured some enemies out of a pā by making a 'whale' from dog-skin cloaks such as the one pictured here. Their enemy hoped to gain whalebone and meat; instead they met defeat.

The traditional lands of the Muriwhenua tribes lie between the Maungataniwha Range in the south and Cape Rēinga in the north. The six tribes are Ngāti Kurī, Ngāi Takoto, Te Pātū, Ngāti Kahu, Te Aupōuri and Te Rarawa.

Cape Reinga

Also known as Te Rerenga Wairua or Te Rēinga, this cape is one of the most sacred Māori places in New Zealand. Tradition says that the spirits of the dead travel along two pathways to Cape Rēinga, at the northernmost tip of the country. One path begins in the south and runs along Te Oneroa-a-Tōhē (Ninety Mile Beach), and the other starts at Kapowairua (Spirits Bay). The spirits congregate at Cape Rēinga before leaping into the water; they surface after crossing the ocean to Manawatāwhi (Three Kings Islands). There they sing a last lament for the loved ones they have left behind before proceeding to their spiritual home in Hawaiki.

Māori Tribes of New Zealand

NGĀPUHI

Uenuku and Kaharau, Rāhiri's warring sons, attached a rope to a kite, and flew it. The path of the kite became the boundary between the Hokianga lands of Kaharau's descendants and the Taumārere lands of Uenuku's people.

> The magical light from Te Ramaroa mountain first guided Kupe into Hokianga Harbour. Many other sacred mountains support the house of Ngāpuhi, a people who played a central role in Māori history.

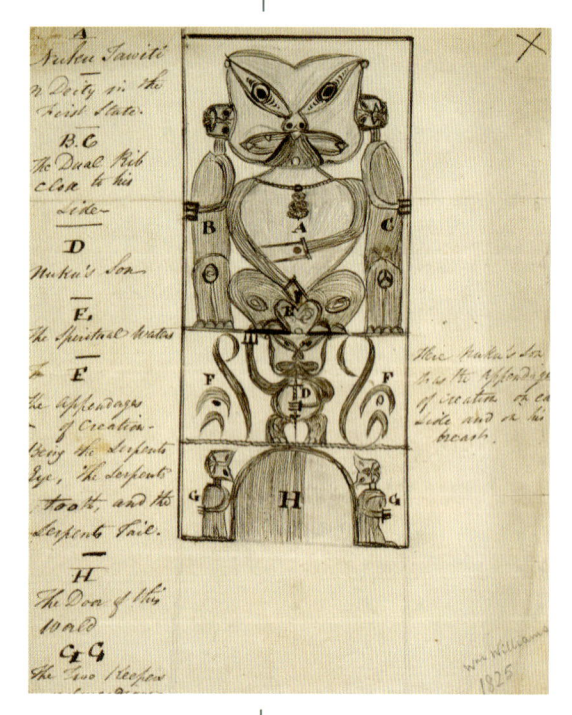

The Ngāpuhi ancestor Nukutawhiti was captain of the Ngātokimatawhaorua canoe. This famous 1824 drawing by the missionary Thomas Kendall shows him in the first state of existence. Kendall's notes and artwork accompanied carvings which were sent to England at the time.

Ngāpuhi is the largest tribe in New Zealand. Their territory stretches from the Hokianga Harbour to the Bay of Islands, and to Whāngārei in the south.

Arriving in the *Matawhaorua* canoe, the navigator Kupe named the Hokianga Harbour. After he returned to Hawaiki, two captains, Nukutawhiti and Ruanui, set off again to establish settlements in New Zealand.

The tribe's founding ancestor, Rāhiri, was descended from Kupe, Nukutawhiti and Puhi. When his two sons fought over land, Rāhiri helped them make peace by flying a kite over the territory. The points where it landed marked the boundary between their two regions – Hokianga and Taumārere.

All tribes north of Auckland are descendants of Kairewa and his wife Waimirirangi, 'the queen of the northern tide'. Through his marriages, Rāhiri forged links with many tribes. Some descendants moved eastward, taking over other groups. Eventually the name of Ngāpuhi was given to all tribes in the Hokianga and Bay of Islands.

EUROPEAN CONTACT

Using muskets gained through trade with Europeans, Ngāpuhi defeated several tribes in the 'musket wars' of the 1820s.

Ngāpuhi chiefs signed both the Declaration of Independence in 1835 and the Treaty of Waitangi in 1840.

But in 1845–46, after chief Hōne Heke protested at growing British control, Ngāpuhi fought the British to a stalemate. Later, they lost much land.

Māori Tribes of New Zealand

The territory of New Zealand's largest tribe stretches from Hokianga to Maunganui Bluff in the west, and from the Bay of Islands to Whāngārei in the east. The map above shows mountains and hills significant to Ngāpuhi as well as the main place names.

When the explorer Kupe left New Zealand to return to Hawaiki, Hokianga Harbour (above right) was his final departure place. Rāhiri, the founding ancestor of Ngāpuhi, was descended from Kupe.

NGĀPUHI TODAY

In 2006 there were more than 122,000 Ngāpuhi people, and more than 50,000 lived in Auckland.

Their central organisation is Te Rūnanga ā Iwi o Ngāpuhi. Renowned descendants include Dame Whina Cooper, who led an important land rights march in 1975.

Rāhiri is the founding ancestor of Ngāpuhi. Hokianga traditions say that Rāhiri's first wife, Āhuaiti, came from this large pā, Pouērua, near Kaikohe, and that she left after a dispute. However, the traditions of her people say that the two were married at Pouērua and that Rāhiri was the one who left.

Māori Tribes of New Zealand 27

WHĀNGĀREI TRIBES

The ocean and coastline were central to the many tribes of Whāngārei. From Muriwhenua down to Auckland, traditions and place names such as Ngunguru (rumbling tides) reflect their seafaring history.

Today, through the Ngāti Wai Trust Board, Māori people of the region are involved in environmental issues such as the preservation of beaches and nearshore islands.

Several tribes belong to the region, including:
- Ngare Raumati
- Ngāi Tāhuhu
- Ngāti Wai
- Te Parawhau.

Ngāti Wai are named after the swirling water (wai) in a cave at the Bay of Islands. Te Parawhau were said to have the largest pā (fortified village) in New Zealand.

The territory of the Whāngārei tribes stretches down the coast from the far north of the North Island to Auckland, and includes Great Barrier and Little Barrier islands. Many tribes lived along the coast, linked by seafaring and trading networks. There are several explanations of how Whāngārei was named. One tradition says that the full name means 'the gathering place of whales'.

ANCESTORS

Among the ancestral canoes from Hawaiki were *Tūnui-a-rangi*, *Te Arawa*, *Moekākara*, *Te Wakatūwhenua*, and *Māhuhu-ki-te-rangi*, captained by Manaia. (Some accounts say he came on the *Ruakaramea*.) His people settled on the coast and the Poor Knights and Hen and Chickens Islands. Manaia is also the name given to the jagged mountain at Whāngārei Harbour.

Puhi, captain of the *Mataatua* canoe, named many places including Matapōuri (darkness), where he landed at night.

There are a number of traditions explaining the jagged outline of Manaia mountain at the entrance to Whāngārei Harbour. One is that the ancestor Manaia and his servant Paeko were both turned into peaks while sparring with each other.

Several ancestral canoes landed on the Whāngārei coast. The Māhuhu-ki-te-rangi canoe landed here at Motu Kōkako (Hole in the Rock), at the entrance to the Bay of Islands.

LAND LOSS

From the 1840s the Whāngārei tribes began to lose much of their territory to the government and to European settlers. In 1890 only 25% of Whāngārei land was owned by Māori, and by 1939 this had fallen to 5%. More land was taken for nature reserves on nearshore islands such as Great Barrier and the Poor Knights.

WHĀNGĀREI TRIBES TODAY

The Ngāti Wai Trust Board assists the Whāngārei tribes in making land claims. It also helps to conserve the local environment and historical sites. Almost 5,000 people said they were affiliated with Ngāti Wai in the 2006 census.

This map shows the main areas of occupation of the Whāngārei tribes and some of the significant places associated with the major canoes of the area.

Ngāti Wai descend from Manaia, captain of the Māhuhu-ki-te-rangi canoe. This carving of him is in the government office of Work and Income in Whāngārei. Today, many Ngāti Wai live close to Whāngārei, both north and south of the city.

Māori Tribes of New Zealand

NGĀTI WHĀTUA

Ngāti Whātua's lands border four harbours – Hokianga, Kaipara, Waitematā and Manukau – and their ancestors include famous warriors and fighters for justice. The Ngāti Whātua story is part of Auckland's story.

Ngāti Whātua consist of four tribes whose lands stretch from the Hokianga down to Auckland. They share a common ancestor called Tuputupuwhenua or Tumutumuwhenua.

They also share a common ancestral canoe, *Māhuhu-ki-te-rangi*. Some say that the captain of the canoe, Rongomai, was drowned when the canoe capsized, then eaten by trevally fish. To this day, his descendants do not eat trevally.

TE ROROA
Te Roroa's name recalls a saying about the bravery of an ancestor, Manumanu II. His enemies said of him, 'Te hei! Te roroa o te tangata, rite tonu ki te kahikatea!' (Behold! That man is as tall as a white pine!) The tribe live in an area known for huge trees; the Waipoua kauri forest is in their territory.

TE URI-O-HAU AND TE TAOŪ
These two tribes are from Kaipara Harbour. Both are descended from Haumoe-whārangi, who was killed in a dispute over kūmara (sweet potato) gardens.

NGĀTI WHĀTUA-O-ŌRĀKEI
Ngāti Whātua-o-Ōrākei conquered the Auckland area in the 1740s. Their leader, Tūperiri, established a pā (fortified village) on One Tree Hill.

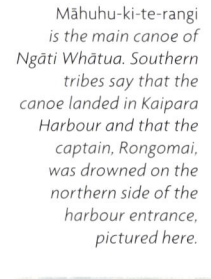

Māhuhu-ki-te-rangi is the main canoe of Ngāti Whātua. Southern tribes say that the canoe landed in Kaipara Harbour and that the captain, Rongomai, was drowned on the northern side of the harbour entrance, pictured here.

Maungakiekie or One Tree Hill is an Auckland landmark. In the 18th century, after conquering the Te Wai-o-Hua tribe led by Kiwi Tāmaki, Ngāti Whātua leader Tūperiri established his pā, Hikurangi, on the hill. The obelisk was erected for the city's centenary in 1940.

WARFARE

In 1807 Ngāti Whātua defeated Ngāpuhi in battle at Moremonui. So many Ngāpuhi people were killed and left on the beach that the battle became known as Te Kai-a-te-karoro — 'food for seagulls'. However, in the 1820s Ngāti Whātua suffered heavy defeats.

EUROPEAN CONTACT

Many Ngāti Whātua leaders signed the Treaty of Waitangi in 1840, but the tribes lost a large amount of land in the next half century. In Auckland, they were left only with land at Ōkahu Bay, and in 1951–52 their houses there were demolished.

Ngāti Whātua-whānui or Ngāti Whātua-tūturu — 'wider' or 'true' Ngāti Whātua — refers to a confederation of four tribes: Te Roroa, Te Uri-o-Hau, Te Taoū, and Ngāti Whātua-o-Ōrākei. This map shows their lands, which span the area between the Hokianga Harbour and Tāmaki (Auckland).

MODERN REVIVAL

In 1977–78 Joe Hawke led a protest against land losses in which a large number of people occupied Auckland's Bastion Point (Takaparawhā). Although the protesters were evicted, the Waitangi Tribunal eventually supported their claims, and also those of Te Roroa. Te Uri-o-Hau and Ngāti Whātua-o-Ōrākei received compensation.

NGĀTI WHĀTUA TODAY

Today, Ngāti Whātua play a prominent role in Auckland life, and in 2006, almost 16,000 people claimed descent from Ngāti Whātua tribes.

Māori Tribes of New Zealand

TĀMAKI TRIBES

Tāmaki (Auckland) is a landscape dominated by volcanoes. In the tradition of one tribe, they were created when the goddess Mahuika sent fire to warm Mataaho, whose wife had left him and taken all his clothes.

In another dramatic version of their creation, the volcanoes were produced when priests chanted spells to send down sun rays, setting the isthmus alight.

Today, the volcanoes are dormant, but Tāmaki's six tribes are very much a part of the cultural landscape.

Tāmaki (Auckland) has been home to a number of iwi (tribes), and today there are six in the region:
- Ngāti Pāoa
- Ngāi Tai
- Te Wai-o-Hua (who originate from Ngā Oho)
- Ngāti Whātua-o-Ōrākei
- Ngāti Te Ata
- Te Kawerau-a-Maki.

Volcanic cones and two harbours, Waitematā and Manukau, dominate the Tāmaki landscape. There are several versions of how Tāmaki got its name. Some believe that the name comes from the ancestor Maki or from one of his daughters, while in another tradition it comes from the 18th-century Te Wai-o-Hua chief Kiwi Tāmaki.

THE CANOES OF TĀMAKI

In early times, canoes were dragged over Te Tō Waka, the narrow stretch of land between the Tāmaki River and Manukau Harbour. From the harbour they went inland along the Waikato River, or they sailed south to Taranaki, or north to Northland. From Waitematā Harbour they travelled east to the Coromandel.

With so many interconnecting routes, Tāmaki is associated with many of the canoes that came during the early migrations from Polynesia.

Kōwhaikiteuru is an important Te Kawerau-a-Maki ancestor. This carving of him at Karekare is by Sunna Thompson, a Te Kawerau-a-Maki artist. Kōwhaikiteuru built the pā Te Kaka Whakaara at Karekare. The Te Kawerau-a-Maki tribe once held land from the Waitākere Ranges north to Leigh.

The crater of Maungawhau (Mt Eden) was called Te Ipu-a-Mataaho (the bowl of Mataaho) because this is where the deity Mataaho lived. It is also said that the other volcanic cones of Auckland were formed when Mataaho's wife left him and took his clothes, so the goddess Mahuika sent fires to warm him.

This map shows the modern locations of the six tribes of the wider Auckland region.

EUROPEAN CONTACT

After Europeans arrived in New Zealand, some tribes acquired guns. During intertribal wars between 1815 and 1840 many Tāmaki tribes suffered heavy losses.

A number of Tāmaki chiefs signed the Treaty of Waitangi in 1840, but this did not ensure that their land was protected. Early European settlement and the relocation of the capital from Russell to Auckland at this time meant land was in demand.

By 1850 most of the usable land in Auckland had been bought by Europeans. Some Māori were driven from their land. Later, land was used for public works such as a sewage plant and Auckland airport.

TĀMAKI TRIBES TODAY

In the mid 1980s the Waitangi Tribunal found that some Tāmaki tribes had lost land unfairly.

Today, having received compensation for losses, the tribes are considered an important part of the future of the Auckland region. In 2006, more than 18,500 people said they were affiliated to the Tāmaki tribes.

Ngāti Te Ata occupied Waiuku and the Āwhitu Peninsula on the southern shores of Manukau Harbour.

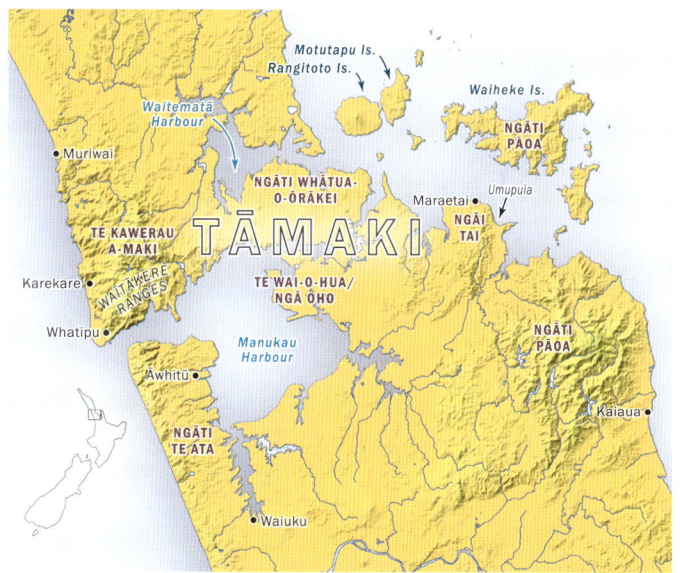

HAURAKI TRIBES

Stretching from Mahurangi, north of Auckland, to Katikati near Tauranga, the Hauraki district has seen the intermingling of many tribes.
Through conflict and war, but also through migration, intermarriage and gifts of land, they have each won a place in this region of harbours, islands and peninsulas.

The white cliffs of the Coromandel coast, above, just south of Whitianga.

The Hauraki region includes the Tāmaki isthmus, Te Hapū-a-Kohe, the Piako, Ōhinemuri and Wairoa districts, the Coromandel Peninsula and Whangamatā.
Although it is dominated by tribes of the Marutūahu confederation, it is also home to many other tribes, including Te Patukirikiri, Ngāti Hako, Ngāti Huarere, Ngāti Hei, Ngāi Tai, Ngāti Pūkenga and Ngāti Rāhiri.

TE PATUKIRIKIRI
The people of Te Patukirikiri were led by the ancestor Kapetaua, who originally belonged to the Wai-o-Hua tribe of the Tāmaki isthmus. They were named after a famous victory on a beach where the only weapons (patu) they had were rocks and stones (kirikiri).

NGĀTI HAKO
Ngāti Hako were the earliest people to settle Hauraki. Their survival among the Marutūahu tribes was ensured when a high-born Ngāti Hako woman, Ruawehea, married Tamaterā, son of the founding ancestor Marutūahu.

NGĀTI HUARERE
The *Te Arawa* canoe landed at various points around the Coromandel Peninsula, and left both people and place names. Ngāti Huarere took their name from Huarere, grandson of Tamatekapua, the captain of *Te Arawa*. Tamatekapua was

buried on Moehau Mountain, which is known as Te Moengahau-o-Tamatekapua (the windy sleeping place of Tamatekapua).

NGĀTI HEI

Ngāti Hei also trace their descent from the *Te Arawa* canoe, and from Hei, the uncle of Tamatekapua. They managed to survive conflicts with the Marutūahu people and Ngāpuhi, and are now located around Te Whitianga-o-Kupe (Whitianga Harbour).

NGĀI TAI

The Ngāi Tai people of Hauraki are related to Ngāi Tai in the Bay of Plenty through three sisters, Te Raukohekohe, Motu-i-tawhiti and Te Kaweinga, who came north and married men from Hauraki. Both Ngāi Tai tribes trace their lines back to the *Tainui* canoe.

NGĀTI PŪKENGA

Ngāti Pūkenga trace their origins to the *Mataatua* canoe. They moved north from Tauranga to the Coromandel Peninsula in the 19th century.

NGĀTI RĀHIRI

The ancestor Rāhiri arrived at Whakatāne on the *Mataatua* canoe, and then accompanied it on its journey north. He later returned to Whakatāne via Hauraki. Members of his party decided to stay in Hauraki, and took the name Ngāti Rāhiri.

HAURAKI TRIBES TODAY

In 2006, more than 3,000 people claimed descent from the Hauraki tribes.

The Hauraki region is dominated by the Marutūahu confederation of tribes. However, Hauraki is also the home of a number of other tribes, including Ngāti Hako, Ngāti Hei, Ngāi Tai, Ngāti Porou, Ngāti Pūkenga, Ngāti Rāhiri and Te Patukirikiri.

Moehau Mountain, one of the major landmarks of the Coromandel Peninsula, is also called Te Moengahau-o-Tamatekapua (the windy sleeping place of Tamatekapua). Tamatekapua was the commander of the Te Arawa canoe, and was buried on the mountain. His grandson, Huarere, gave his name to the tribe Ngāti Huarere of the Hauraki region.

MARUTŪAHU TRIBES

> The five sons of Marutūahu gave rise to the five tribes that dominate the Hauraki region.
> For centuries a unique grove of trees at Waihīhī symbolised the fertility of the area. Other icons still survive: the stone mauri (effigy) of Marutūahu, and the carved meeting house Hotunui, at Auckland Museum.

The five tribes of the Marutūahu confederation are:
- Ngāti Rongoū
- Ngāti Tamaterā
- Ngāti Whanaunga
- Ngāti Maru
- Ngāti Pāoa.

These peoples are all descended from the ancestor Marutūahu, who came from Kāwhia on the west coast of the North Island.

Before Marutūahu was born, his father Hotunui had fallen out with his father-in-law. Hotunui went to live in the Hauraki region, where he was treated badly by the local people. When Marutūahu grew up he wanted to restore his father's reputation. He went to Hauraki, conquered the local people, and settled there.

ORIGIN OF THE MARUTŪAHU TRIBES

Marutūahu married two sisters. The children of these two marriages became the ancestors of the tribes who eventually conquered the whole Hauraki region, including the Tāmaki isthmus, the Wairoa, Piako and Ōhinemuri districts, the Coromandel Peninsula (Moehau) and Whangamatā.

Marutūahu's ambitious second son, Tamaterā, gave his name to the dominant tribe, Ngāti Tamaterā. The eldest son, Tamatepō, was the ancestor of the Ngāti Rongoū people. Because Tamatepō was overshadowed by Tamaterā, his descendants did not achieve prominence until the

This view near Te Kōuma looks north-west over Coromandel Harbour, in the tribal region of the Marutūahu people.

time of his grandson, Rongomai. Whanaunga, Marutūahu's third son, was the ancestor of Ngāti Whanaunga.

Marutūahu's eldest son from his second marriage was Te Ngako. Te Ngako married his half-brother Tamaterā's daughter. After further intermarriage between the families of Te Ngako and Tamaterā, the ancestor Rautao was born, and the tribe of Ngāti Maru emerged. Ngāti Pāoa took their name from the Waikato ancestor Pāoa, who married a granddaughter of Tamaterā.

HAURAKI RESOURCES

The Hauraki region is rich in gold, timber and marine resources. The first two were exploited by European settlers. In recent times the Marutūahu people have established successful enterprises such as mussel farms, and are involved in the management of the Hauraki Gulf Maritime Park and forest reserves.

MARUTŪAHU TRIBES TODAY

In the 2006 census, almost 10,000 people claimed descent from the Marutūahu tribes.

The Hauraki region stretches from Mahurangi in the north to Ngā Kurī-a-Whārei (near Katikati) in the south. This region is dominated by the Marutūahu confederation of tribes, which are Ngāti Rongoū, Ngāti Tamaterā, Ngāti Whanaunga, Ngāti Maru and Ngāti Pāoa.

Opposite: Ureia was the taniwha who lived in Tīkapa (the Firth of Thames). Accounts differ as to the form Ureia took — some say he was a fish, others a school of fish. Either way, Ureia was a powerful symbol of the fertility and mana of the Hauraki region. Ureia was killed at Pūponga, by the Manukau Harbour. This carving of him is located inside the Hotunui meeting house, which once stood at Thames and is now in the Auckland Museum.

Māori Tribes of New Zealand 37

WAIKATO

> Home of the Māori King movement, the lush Waikato region is the territory of numerous tribes descended from the people of the *Tainui* canoe.
> Key roles in their story have been played by women: the ancestor Kahu, who as a widow named many landmarks on a journey of grieving; Te Puea, founder of the Tūrangawaewae marae; and the late queen, Dame Te Ātairangikaahu.

The large Waikato group of tribes are descended from the people of the *Tainui* canoe, and take their name from the Waikato River, New Zealand's longest. Their region stretches north from the Mōkau River in Taranaki to the Tāmaki isthmus where Auckland city now stands. Kāwhia, on the west coast, has special importance because it was the final resting place of the *Tainui*, and the first homeland of the Waikato peoples.

When her husband died, the ancestor Kahu made a famous journey from Kāwhia to Hauraki. Along the way she named landmarks such as the mountain Pirongia (Te Pirongia o Te Aroaro ō Kahu – the scented pathway of Kahu). Two other important ancestors are Tūheitia and his son Māhanga, who were both great warriors. Māhanga gave his name to a Waikato tribe, Ngāti Māhanga.

THE KING MOVEMENT

As more British settlers arrived in the 1850s, Māori people around New Zealand decided to choose their own king, to show their unity and control of the land. The King movement became linked with the Waikato people because the first king chosen was the Waikato chief Pōtatau Te Wherowhero. His descendants have continued to take on the role of king or queen. In 2010 the king was Tūheitia Paki, son of the late queen, Dame Te Ātairangikaahu.

Tūheitia was the father of Māhanga, the ancestor of Ngāti Māhanga, an important Tainui and Waikato tribe. Tūheitia was killed through trickery while out at sea. He became a taniwha and came to reside in the Waipā River. In this carving, outside the Novotel Tainui hotel in Hamilton, Tūheitia is depicted with a fish-like tail, to signify his transformation into a taniwha.

This is the river mouth at Port Waikato. The name 'Waikato' comes from an incident when the Tainui canoe arrived just off the mouth of the river. The current could be seen exerting a pull (kato) in the sea — so the river was named Waikato (wai meaning water).

38   Māori Tribes of New Zealand

This is the Waikato River, with Taupiri mountain at left, on the bend of the river. Taupiri is the sacred mountain of the Waikato people. Many Waikato ancestors and chiefs are buried on Taupiri, including all the Māori kings, and the late queen, Dame Te Ātairangikaahu.

A famous saying that describes the region of the Tainui peoples begins: 'Mōkau is above, Tāmaki is below'. Accordingly, this map, which shows the area settled by tribes who trace their descent from the voyagers of the Tainui canoe, is oriented south to north. The map also shows the route and landing places of the canoe within Tainui territory, and the places of significance to the Tainui people. The Tainui canoe first landed at Whangaparāoa in the Bay of Plenty.

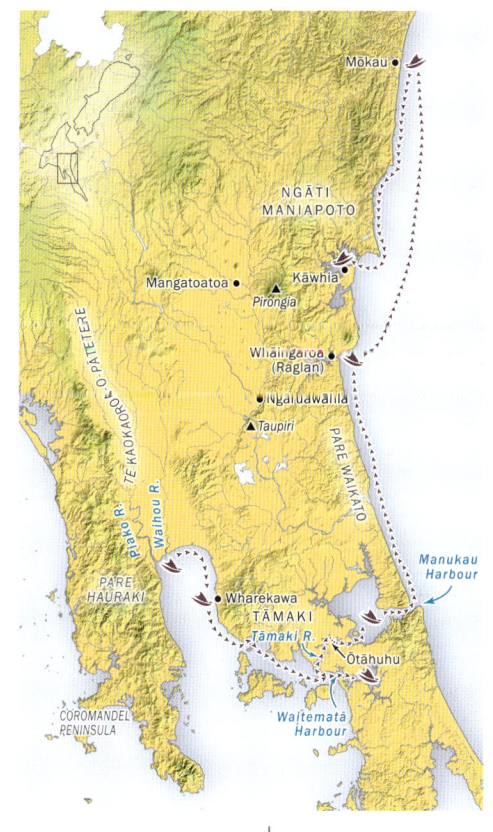

WAR IN WAIKATO

At first the New Zealand government was suspicious of the King movement, and wanted the fertile Waikato land for the European settlers.

In 1863 soldiers invaded the Waikato, and although the tribes fought fiercely, they could not stop the troops pushing south. The final battle was at Ōrākau, south of Te Awamutu, in 1864.

Māori defenders made their last stand with the famous cry, 'Ka whawhai tonu mātou, ake, ake, ake!' (We shall fight on forever!). They were forced into exile in what became known as the King Country, and the government confiscated the Waikato lands.

REVIVAL

In the 1920s and 1930s Te Puea Hērangi, the granddaughter of the second king, led the Waikato people in building the Tūrangawaewae marae at Ngaruawahia. This is now the centre of the King movement.

WAIKATO TRIBES TODAY

The late queen and her brother, Sir Robert Mahuta, brought the Waikato raupatu (confiscation) claim to conclusion in 1995. The government gave the Waikato people compensation for past wrongs, and an apology. They have since set up a college and health services, and have many marae, businesses and other projects in the Waikato.

In 2006, almost 33,500 people were affiliated with the Waikato tribes. More than 11,000 lived in Auckland.

Māori Tribes of New Zealand

NGĀTI MANIAPOTO

*'Kia mau tonu ki tēnā; kia mau ki te kawau mārō.
   Whanake ake! Whanake ake!'*
'Stick to that, the straight-flying cormorant!'

These were the instructions of the dying ancestor Maniapoto to his people. Such strength of purpose characterises their history, including early economic success, protecting the King Country, and preserving their culture.

Te Kūiti in the central North Island lies at the heart of Ngāti Maniapoto territory. The western boundary is the coast from Kāwhia down to Mōkau. To the east is the Rangitoto Range. It was believed that lightning over the range was a sign of death.

Ngāti Maniapoto trace their lineage back to the *Tainui* canoe, and particularly to Tūrongo.

The ancestor Maniapoto lived in the 17th century. In a famous incident his father, the chief Rereahu, passed on his sacred power to Maniapoto, although the usual custom was to hand it to the oldest son. Rereahu told Maniapoto to bite the crown of his head, which was painted with red ochre. Maniapoto's red lips were a clear sign that he was the chosen chief.

Settlements were clustered around harbours and fertile river valleys such as the Waipā, said to be the home of Waiwaia, the tribal guardian.

THE COMING OF THE PĀKEHĀ

Some European settlers married prominent women of the tribe, producing several important Pākehā–Māori families. A Frenchman, Louis Hetet, married Paeata, a chief's daughter, and in the 20th century one of their descendants, Rangimārie Hetet, became famous as a skilled weaver.

At the drop of a hat
It is said that the second Māori king, Tāwhiao, threw his hat over a map of the North Island and declared his rule over the area it landed on. Thus the King Country, or Rohe Pōtae (area of the hat), was named.

This carving of the ancestor Maniapoto is from the meeting house Te Kohaarua, at Maniaroa marae, Mōkau. Maniapoto is depicted living in his cave.

40   Māori Tribes of New Zealand

In his last years Maniapoto lived in a cave in the limestone region of Waitomo. A large eel which lived in the stream below the cave was adopted as a pet by the old man, and thus escaped the normal fate reserved for fine fat eels.

THE MĀORI KING MOVEMENT

In 1857 the tribe supported the establishment of a Māori king as part of their effort to stop settlers buying up their land. They set up a boundary around the King Country, or Te Rohe Pōtae, to keep out Europeans. This remained until 1883.

NGĀTI MANIAPOTO TODAY

In 2006 this large tribe had over 33,000 members, with the central marae at Te Kūiti. Many have moved away from the ancestral lands, but the Maniapoto Māori Trust Board ensures the tribe's identity and interests are protected. Every two years many people return home to attend a sporting festival and celebrate being Maniapoto.

This map shows the traditional lands of Ngāti Maniapoto.

Ko Tainui te waka; Ko Hoturoa te tangata! (Tainui is the canoe; Hoturoa is the man!). As this proverb implies, Hoturoa was the commander of the Tainui canoe and the ancestor of the Tainui people. In this post at the Ōtāwhao marae, Hoturoa is shown hauling in the anchor of his canoe.

Māori Tribes of New Zealand   41

TE ARAWA

Many of those who first arrived on the *Te Arawa* canoe became great explorers, founding tribal groups across the North Island's dramatic geothermal zone. Although there were many conflicts, peace was often settled through marriages.

One famous love story is that of the beautiful Hinemoa, who lived on the shores of Lake Rotorua, and Tūtānekai on Mokoia Island, who would play his flute to her at night.

This carving is of Houmaitawhiti. According to tradition, his son Tamatekapua set sail for New Zealand from Hawaiki.

The traditional lands of the Te Arawa people are around the Rotorua lakes. Te Arawa tribes today include:
- Ngāti Pikiao
- Tūhourangi
- Ngāti Whakaue.

In Te Arawa tradition, the ancestor Tamatekapua and his relatives set out for New Zealand from Hawaiki in a double-hulled canoe. After a shark rescued the crew from being eaten by a huge sea creature, the people renamed their canoe – and themselves – *Te Arawa*, after a species of shark.

Tamatekapua and his people explored the North Island's coast by canoe before settling in Maketū, in the western Bay of Plenty. Some of the group, including the explorer Īhenga, travelled south and settled around the Rotorua lakes, where they were able to use the geothermally heated water and steam, as well as the lakes' fresh water.

Rangitihi was an important ancestor. His eight children and their descendants became known as Ngā Pūmanawa e Waru (the eight beating hearts).

Competition among Ngāti Pikiao, Tūhourangi and Ngāti Whakaue sparked conflict within Te Arawa. These disputes were sometimes settled though marriages, and the groups also banded together to fight enemy tribes.

In 1823 Ngāpuhi, led by Hongi Hika and armed with muskets, attacked Te Arawa. The tribe took refuge on Mokoia Island in Lake Rotorua, armed only with traditional weapons. The invaders took them by surprise, and there was a great loss of lives.

In the 1860s Te Arawa fought alongside the government against the tribes of Waikato and the East Coast, and against guerrilla leader Te Kooti. But some of the tribe's lands were lost after the wars.

TOURISM AND VOLCANOES

The area's dramatic scenery and geothermal attractions drew many visitors in the 19th century. Te Arawa people often acted as guides, and Ngāti Whakaue leased land to the government to build the spa town of Rotorua.

When Mt Tarawera erupted in 1886, the famous Pink and White Terraces at Rotomahana were destroyed.

The tourist guide Sophia Hinerangi had seen a mysterious phantom canoe on Lake Tarawera shortly before the eruption – often considered to be a premonition of the disaster.

TE ARAWA TODAY

After the Second World War, many Te Arawa drifted to the cities in search of work. In 2006, there were more than 51,000 Te Arawa people. More than 10,000 lived in Auckland.

Te Arawa's claim to the Waitangi Tribunal concerning the Rotorua lakes was settled in 2006 with an apology from the Crown and a recognition of Te Arawa's mana (authority) over the lakes.

Mt Tarawera, seen here across Lake Tarawera, erupted ferociously in June 1886, burying Lake Rotomahana, its terraces and over 150 Tūhourangi and Ngāti Rangitihi residents. Protected by a valley, the village of Te Wairoa was distant enough for most residents to survive.

On arrival in New Zealand the Te Arawa people explored the Bay of Plenty to the far eastern reaches of Whangaparāoa (Cape Runaway) and to the inner harbours of Waitematā (Hauraki Gulf). The people soon moved inland toward the geothermal areas around the Rotorua lakes.

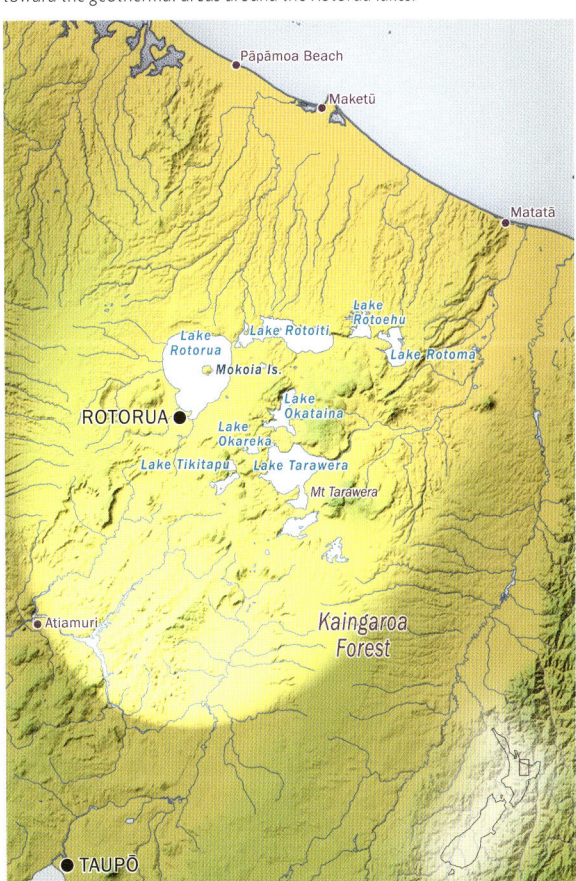

NGĀTI TŪWHARETOA

Among the heroes and heroines of Ngāti Tūwharetoa legend are the beautiful mountains and lakes of the central North Island. New Zealand's biggest lake, Taupō, lies at the heart of the tribe's homeland.

Ngāti Tūwharetoa's traditional lands are around Lake Taupō. Crayfish, whitebait, fish and eels were once plentiful in the lakes and rivers. But in the 1900s, trout were introduced to the lake, and have almost destroyed the native species.

ANCESTRAL EXPLORERS

Arriving in the *Te Arawa* canoe, the high priest Ngātoroirangi travelled south from Maketū and claimed land that became Ngāti Tūwharetoa's ancestral home. Ngātoroirangi nearly lost his life while climbing the chilly slopes of Mt Tongariro. After warming himself with a basket of fire, he threw it onto the mountain and created the hot springs known as Ketetahi (meaning 'one basket'). Another ancestor from the *Te Arawa* was the explorer, Tia. His name has been given to many landmarks, including the Aratiatia rapids (the stairway of Tia).

TŪWHARETOA

The tribe takes its name from Tūwharetoa, a 16th-century chief who lived near Kawerau. He was famed as a warrior, carver and scholar. This handsome leader married three times and attracted many beautiful women.

Tūwharetoa's sons established the tribe's authority in the Taupō region. At the end of the 18th century the warrior Herea became recognised as the paramount chief. His family took the name Te Heuheu from a māheuheu shrub which once hid a family burial place. Since then the Te Heuheu family has provided the tribe's paramount chiefs.

Ngāti Tūwharetoa trace their origins to the Te Arawa canoe. Ngātoroirangi, the high priest on the canoe, had strained relations with the captain, Tamatekapua. So on arrival he set off inland to claim new lands for his descendants. This carving of Ngātoroirangi is at the Wellington office of Tūwharetoa Ltd Finance Company.

44   Māori Tribes of New Zealand

The mountains Tongariro, Ngāuruhoe and Ruapehu, which today form part of Tongariro National Park, were gifted to the government by Horonuku Te Heuheu in 1887.

TONGARIRO NATIONAL PARK

According to tradition, there were once four mountains in the centre of the North Island: Tongariro, Taranaki (Mt Egmont), Tauhara and Pūtauaki (Mt Edgecumbe). They fought for the affections of the beautiful mountain Pīhanga. Tongariro won, and the others fled west, north and east, where they stand today.

In 1887 Horonuku Te Heuheu gifted the lands south of Lake Taupō to the government, and they became Tongariro National Park.

NGĀTI TŪWHARETOA TODAY

In the 2006 census, almost 35,000 people said they were descended from Ngāti Tūwharetoa.

> **Born too late**
> The chief Horonuku, descended from Herea, was convinced that his first child would be a boy, so he blew a trumpet heralding its arrival. In fact, the child was a girl. When a boy did arrive two years later there was no trumpet sound, and the boy was named Tūreiti – a transliteration of 'too late'.

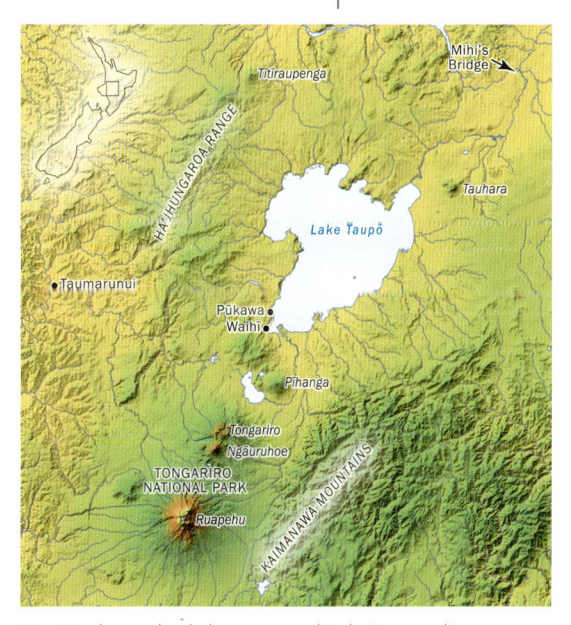

Ngāti Tūwharetoa's tribal area surrounds Lake Taupō and is bounded by Mihi's Bridge in the north, the Hauhungaroa Range in the west, the Kaimanawa Mountains in the east and Tongariro National Park in the south.

Māori Tribes of New Zealand   45

TAURANGA MOANA TRIBES

At the entrance to Tauranga Harbour in the Bay of Plenty, the volcanic cone of Mt Maunganui – originally Mauao – presides over the territory of the Tauranga Moana iwi (tribes).

Linked through a long history of migration, wars and allegiances, they won a famous victory against British troops in 1864. The battle of Gate Pā remains a testament to the courage and ingenuity of the tribes of Tauranga.

Mauao (Mt Maunganui), above, is the sacred mountain at the entrance to Tauranga Harbour.

There are three iwi of Tauranga Moana (Tauranga Harbour):

NGĀTI RANGINUI
Ngāti Ranginui's territory includes the Tauranga shoreline. Their ancestor is Ranginui, a great-grandson of the Polynesian navigator Tamatea.

NGĀI TE RANGI
The name is shortened from that of their chief, Te Rangihouhiri, after he was killed in battle at Maketū. To avenge his death, they successfully fought for land at Tauranga Moana.

NGĀTI PŪKENGA
Ngāti Pūkenga occupy land at Ngāpeke, and Manaia in Hauraki. It is said that their ancestor Pūkenga named the Kaimai Ranges.

The boundaries of the tribes' territory run from Bowentown, at Tauranga Harbour, down to Pāpāmoa, inland along the Kaimai Ranges, and back to Bowentown.

In tradition, Mt Maunganui, at the harbour's edge, was once a nameless peak in the Hautere forest. Spurned by the beautiful mountain Pūwhenua, he asked the forest fairies to drag him into the ocean, to dull his pain. But at sunrise they fled, leaving him forever at the shore.

His ancient name is Mauao – 'caught in the light of day'.

CANOES
The people of the region trace their descent from three Polynesian canoes:

TE ARAWA
A crew member, Hei, laid claim to the district as the canoe sailed past.

TĀKITIMU
It is said that only people of high rank travelled on this canoe. Tamatea was the captain, who named Mt Maunganui. Ngāti Ranginui are among his descendants.

MATAATUA
Muriwai, sister of the captain of this canoe, moved to Tauranga Moana. When her two children drowned there she marked the sacred tribal boundaries which remain today. Ngāi Te Rangi and Ngāti Pūkenga are descended from this canoe.

This map shows the tribal boundaries of the three Tauranga Moana tribes, Ngāti Ranginui, Ngāi Te Rangi and Ngāti Pūkenga. Their coastal boundaries extend from Bowentown to Pāpāmoa, while inland they reach from the Ōtawa mountains to the Kaimai Range.

THE BATTLE OF GATE PĀ
In 1864 British troops were sent to block support for the Māori King among the people of Tauranga. Facing attack, the 250-strong tribal force hid in trenches dug at Pukehinahina, now called Gate Pā. After constant bombardment, the unseen warriors opened fire and defeated the attack. But weeks later, the British attacked again at Te Ranga, killing many. Large areas of land were then taken for European settlement.

TAURANGA MOANA TRIBES TODAY
With more than 21,500 people in 2006, the Tauranga Moana tribes work hard to maintain their language and resources in this fast growing urban area.

Victory from the bunkers
The battle of Gate Pā was one of the few outright Māori victories against the British during the wars over land. The Māori warriors waited in reinforced bunkers, strong enough to withstand the bombardment. The pā itself was designed as a trap to draw in the British troops. After the wars were over, the British army used the fortifications at Gate Pā as a model for trenching, and some have said that such fortifications were a precursor of 'trench warfare' used in the First World War.

This is one of seven carvings by James Tapiata, on the Strand, the main street of Tauranga. The carvings represent the stars of Matariki – the Pleiades – whose arrival marks the Māori new year. This carving is of Ururangi, one of the stars. It is a symbol of the close connection between the Tauranga and Waikato people, forged particularly by Waikato's involvement in the battles of Gate Pā and Te Ranga. The carving, in traditional Tainui style, features the Waikato River.

NGĀTI AWA

Ngāti Awa have a motto:
'I am like a fledgling, a newborn bird just learning to fly.'

These dying words of the chief Te Mautaranui bring hope for a bright future. Having lost their tribal land in the wars of the mid-1860s, Ngāti Awa are now putting grievances behind them.

A trust board, a centre of higher learning and a radio station are all signs of new life in a modern context.

The traditional tribal area of Ngāti Awa is in the Bay of Plenty. The boundaries of the Mataatua tribes are from Bowentown in the west to Whangaparāoa in the east. Muriwai, sister of the *Mataatua* captain Toroa, placed a restriction on this area of the coast when her two children were drowned – 'mai i Ngā Kurī-a-Whārei-ki-Tihirau' (from the Dogs of Whārei to Tihirau). Pūtauaki (Mt Edgecumbe) is the tribe's ancestral mountain.

ORIGINS

Ngāti Awa trace their origins from important early ancestors:
- Māui, the legendary hero who was half man and half god
- Tīwakawaka, the first explorer to settle the land around Whakatāne
- Toi, who lived at Kaputerangi above Whakatāne.

Ngāti Awa tradition tells of the arrival of the *Mataatua* canoe, captained by Toroa. His grandson, Awanuiarangi II, became the ancestor from whom Ngāti Awa and their sub-tribes all claim descent.

The tribe began in the north of New Zealand, but around 1600 they migrated south. Tītahi led one group down the west coast to Waitara in Taranaki; the other group, led by Kauri, travelled down the east coast to Tauranga.

The rock Turuturu-Roimata is just off the coast from the landing place of the Mataatua canoe. The statue on the top of the rock depicts Wairaka, the daughter of Toroa, captain of the canoe. When the canoe started drifting back out to sea she is said to have saved it by grabbing a paddle and crying out 'Kia whakatāne au i ahau!' (I will act like a man). This incident is said to be the origin of Whakatāne's name. The island in the distance is Moutohorā or Whale Island.

THE 19TH AND 20TH CENTURIES

Initially, Ngāti Awa and European settlers were quite friendly. However, the settlers began to want land and the tribe became more protective of their territory.

Eventually Ngāti Awa were accused of rebellion and blamed for the death of the government agent James Fulloon. Their land was confiscated as a result.

NGĀTI AWA TODAY

In the late 20th century a Ngāti Awa tribal authority was established, as well as a centre of higher learning and a radio station.

Ngāti Awa are also repairing the Mataatua meeting house, an important cultural and historical icon. A settlement agreement was made with the Crown for past grievances in 2003.

In the 2006 census, 15,258 people considered themselves to be of Ngāti Awa descent.

The work above, 'He tātāi kōrero o ngā iwi o Te Awa' (the knowledge and traditional history of the Ngāti Awa and Te Āti Awa people), records the shared histories of the two tribes. It was prepared by students of Te Whare Wānanga of Awanuiarangi. The carved figure in the middle represents Toitehuatahi (Toi) – likened to Professor Raumati Gary Hook, the former chief executive of the whare wānanga – fishing up a degree. On the left is Awanuiarangi I, an important ancestor of both tribes. The carving on the right is of Toroa, captain of the Mataatua canoe, and Awanuiarangi II, the great-grandson of Toroa, and Ngāti Awa's founding ancestor.

Within the domain of the Mataatua canoe, the Ngāti Awa people are to be found in an area centred on Whakatāne. This map shows the Ngāti Awa lands and some of the places of significance to the tribe.

Ngāti Awa people live on the Rangitāiki Plain. This view (right) looking west shows the Whakatāne River mouth in the foreground. The sandspit in the middle of the picture is the Ōpihi Spit, an important Ngāti Awa burial site.

Māori Tribes of New Zealand

TE WHAKATŌHEA

'Tangohia mai te taura i taku kakī kia waiata au i taku waiata.'
'Take the rope from my throat that I may sing my song.'

These words were sung by Mokomoko, wrongly accused in 1865 of the murder of a missionary. As punishment for his death the government took much of Te Whakatōhea's territory. With a harbour rich in fish and shellfish, and forests offering fern grounds, eel fisheries and pigeons, that land seemed like paradise lost.

Today, the tribe has new assets, and is poised to negotiate further settlements.

Te Whakatōhea territory includes Ōhiwa Harbour in the eastern Bay of Plenty. Ōpōtiki lies at the centre.

The area was rich in food resources. Mussels and crayfish abounded in Ōhiwa Harbour, and in the forests it was easy to catch fat kererū (wood pigeons) and other native birds. There are many important ancestors:

TARAWA
Tarawa was the first to arrive from Hawaiki (the Polynesian homeland) – it is believed that he swam from Polynesia to Paerātā.

TAUTŪRANGI
Tautūrangi came in the *Nukutere* canoe, which he moored to a white rock named Te Rangi.

MURIWAI
Muriwai, a female ancestor, arrived in the *Mataatua* canoe. Ōpōtiki tradition says she seized the paddles and saved the canoe from drifting out to sea, calling out, 'Me whakatāne au i ahau!' ('I must act like a man!') Whakatāne is named after her act.

KAHUKI
Kahuki was a celebrated leader of the Whakatāne sub-tribe.

In 1993 the justice minister Doug Graham apologised to Te Whakatōhea and the descendants of Mokomoko. Mokomoko was wrongfully accused and hanged for the murder of the missionary Carl Völkner in 1865. Shown here is Hiona St Stephen's Church, which was completed in 1864 for Völkner. He was buried beside the church. When the full pardon was given to Mokomoko, it was placed in the church for safekeeping and as a symbol of reconciliation between Māori and Pākehā.

This greenstone adze, known as Waiwharangi, is an important Te Whakatōhea trophy of war. It was exchanged for the head of the Ngāti Tai chief, Tūterangikūrei. Waiwharangi is now kept in the Whakatāne Museum.

50 Māori Tribes of New Zealand

BATTLES

There was much bloodshed as the people fought neighbouring tribes. In one of the last attacks, Te Whakatōhea warriors exchanged the head of an enemy chief killed in battle for the return of a prized greenstone adze. The adze, named Waiwharangi, is now held in the Whakatāne Museum.

When European missionaries arrived in the 19th century, there was a period of peace. Carl Völkner was a German missionary at Ōpōtiki. He became unpopular among Te Whakatōhea, who believed he was a government spy. When he was killed for spying in 1865, the government took large areas of Te Whakatōhea land. Nearly 100 years later the people received compensation for this injustice.

TE WHAKATŌHEA TODAY

The tribe consists of six sub-tribes: Ngāti Ruatakena, Ngāti Patumoana, Ngāti Ngahere, Ngāi Tamahaua, Ngāti Ira and Te Ūpokorehe. The Te Whakatōhea Māori Trust Board holds farmland and provides training in horticulture and other skills. In 2006, Te Whakatōhea had more than 12,000 people.

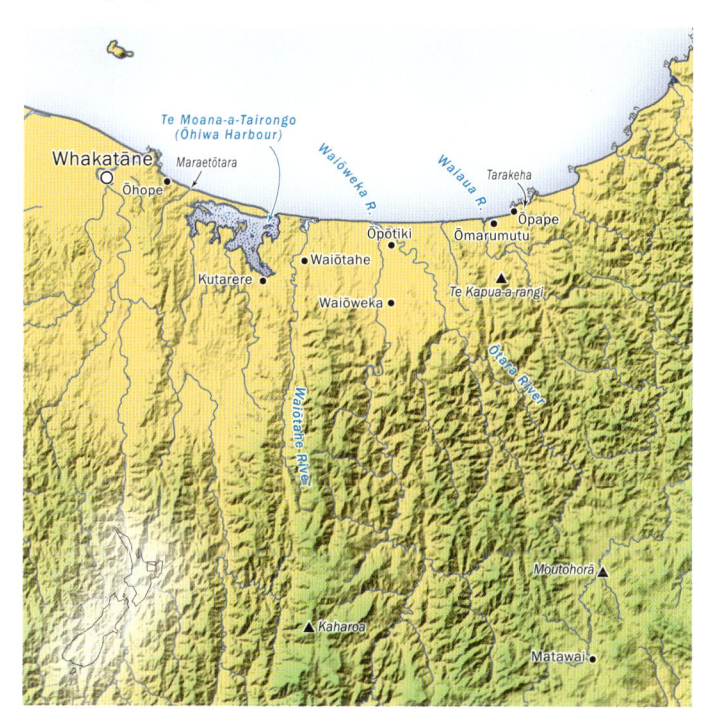

Te Whakatōhea's six sub-tribes live in an area bordered by the eastern Bay of Plenty coastline. This extends from Ōhiwa Harbour to Ōpape. Inland, it follows a south-east angle to Matawai.

Like totem poles, two pouwhenua or pou stand side by side on the beach at Paerātā, their carvings telling Te Whakatōhea and Pākehā stories. Both were carved by Heke Collier. The first, shown right, tells the story of Tarawa, who sailed with his brother Tāwharanui from Hawaiki. They brought two pet tānahanaha fish and released them in a small spring close by. The spring became known as Ōpōtiki-mai-tawhiti, 'two pets from afar', and the name of Ōpōtiki township recalls the event. The carving also shows the two voyaging canoes, Te Arautauta and Te Tohorā.

Māori Tribes of New Zealand 51

NGĀI TŪHOE

Isolated high up in the rugged Urewera country, with little useable land, Ngāi Tūhoe developed a powerful connection with the mountains, forests and rivers.

They say that their ancestors were Te Maunga (the Mountain) and Hine-pūkohu-rangi (the Mist Maiden) – personifications of the natural world, who brought forth the people known as Ngāi Tūhoe.

Maungapōhatu is the sacred mountain of Ngāi Tūhoe. In times long ago, there lived a woman called Hine-pūkohu-rangi, the personification of mist and fog, who enticed Te Maunga (the mountain) to earth. From their union came Pōtiki I, the ancestor of Ngā Pōtiki, one of the tribes occupying the land before the arrival of the Mataatua canoe. And so Tūhoe claim they are descended from their environment: the rugged bush ranges of the Urewera and the white mist clouds that cover them.

When the *Mataatua* canoe arrived in the Bay of Plenty, the voyagers found three tribes already living there – Ngā Pōtiki, Te Tini o Toi and Te Hapū-oneone. The *Mataatua* sailed north with most of the crew, leaving only the captain, Toroa, and his family. They intermarried with the original people and over time the Tūhoe people emerged.

The tribe take their name from Tūhoe-pōtiki (or Tūhoe), a great-grandson of Toroa. He and his brothers fought over the land and resources; Tūhoe won. He settled and eventually died at Kāwhia on the North Island's west coast, but his descendants remained on the land in Te Urewera.

TE UREWERA TERRITORY

The Tūhoe region is heavily forested, steep country, with fast-running, north-flowing rivers. The people lived mostly in river valleys and small forest clearings. As there was little farming land, they relied on the forests for food, clothing and shelter. They moved from place to place as the seasons changed. Maungapōhatu is the sacred mountain, and Lake Waikaremoana is 'the bathing waters of the ancestors'.

THE WARS OF THE 1860s AND EARLY 1870s

Because they lived so far from centres of trade, Tūhoe contact with Europeans came much later than for other tribes. But they did trade with other Māori for European goods such as livestock and seeds. Their first major contact with Europeans came during the wars of the 1860s. Tūhoe fought the government in the battle of Ōrākau in 1864. They were wrongly accused of being in rebellion when the missionary Carl Völkner was killed in Ōpōtiki, and their fertile lands were taken. Worse was to follow when government troops invaded Te Urewera in search of Te Kooti Arikirangi, a prophet and resistance leader from the East Coast.

Te Kooti began a campaign against government forces in Poverty Bay in 1868. Tūhoe people sheltered and supported him. In response, the government destroyed their homes. After the suffering caused by the wars, the tribe closed their doors to the outside world. They refused to survey, lease or sell their land, and forbade the building of roads.

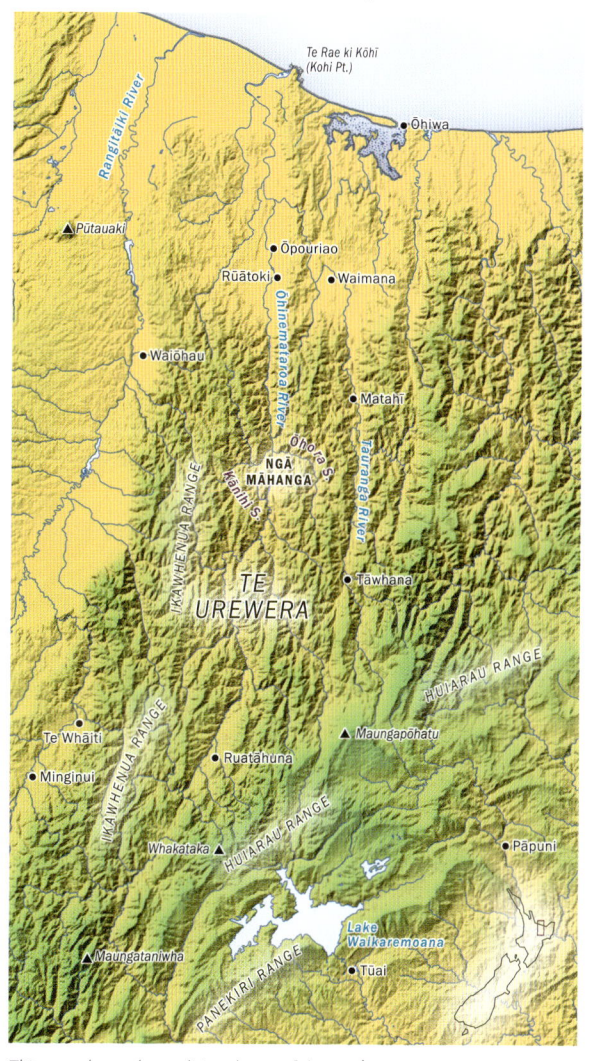

RELIGION

Many Tūhoe belong to Ringatū, the faith started by Te Kooti. In the early 1900s a new religious leader, Rua Kēnana, started a thriving community at Maungapōhatu, to which people from many tribes were drawn. The government was suspicious of his teachings and activities, and in 1916 he was arrested and imprisoned.

NGĀI TŪHOE TODAY

Every two years, Tūhoe people from around New Zealand gather to celebrate their heritage at Te Hui Ahurei. Tūhoe still live and hunt for food in Te Urewera. One of the challenges the tribe faces is to maintain their identity in a changing world. In the 2006 census, 32,670 people claimed Ngāi Tūhoe descent.

This map shows the traditional area of the Tūhoe people, with important mountain ranges, rivers and settlements marked.

Tūhoe children stand in front of Tāne-nui-a-Rangi meeting house at Maungapōhatu, on New Year's Day 2004. They are holding the flag of Te Mana Motuhake o Tūhoe, a group active in highlighting issues important to the tribe.

TE WHĀNAU-Ā-APANUI

Fortune favoured Apanui Ringamutu, the founding ancestor of Te Whānau-ā-Apanui. As a young boy he was given territory on the East Coast, including the Mōtū River. His many descendants cultivated these lands, and put profits from whaling back into their community.

Today Te Whānau-ā-Apanui manages fisheries, forestry blocks and other successful ventures.

Te Whānau-ā-Apanui's tribal territory is a strip of the East Coast from Te Taumata-ō-Apanui to Pōtaka. Whakaari (White Island) and the mountain Whanokao remain significant to the people.

APANUI RINGAMUTU

Apanui's mother Rongomaihuatahi was descended from Porourangi of the *Horouta* canoe, who was a founder of Ngāti Porou. His father Tūrīrangi was a descendant of Tamatekapua of the *Te Arawa* canoe, and the Ngāriki people of the *Tauira* canoe. When Rongomaihuatahi took Apanui to meet his relatives at Ōmāio, they gave land to the boy. Because of his noble ancestry, the people in that area were named after him: Te Whānau-ā-Apanui (the family of Apanui).

Apanui had four wives and many children and grandchildren. His son Tūkākī is commemorated in the meeting house at Te Kaha. Tūkākī's son Tamahae became the tribe's greatest warrior.

WHALING AND FARMING

In the 1820s and 1830s, European whalers taught the local people how to catch whales. This became a major industry for Te Whānau-ā-Apanui in the early 20th century. Whales were hauled ashore, then boiled down in big tri-pots to produce whale oil. The smell was terrible, but everyone enjoyed the meat.

In the 1900s, land was cleared for cattle, sheep and dairy farms. Over the years, three

This carving of Apanui Ringamutu, the founding ancestor of Te Whānau-ā-Apanui, is in Te Hono ki Hawaiki, the marae at the Museum of New Zealand Te Papa Tongarewa. It was carved by a team under the direction of the well-known Te Whānau-ā-Apanui artist Cliff Whiting.

tribal members won the Ahuwhenua Cup, awarded for achievements in farming. But during the 1980s, small farms struggled to survive.

TE WHĀNAU-Ā-APANUI TODAY

During the 20th century, many people left for opportunities in the cities or overseas. But others remain in their tribal region, and since the 1990s the governing body (Te Rūnanga o te Whānau) has run a fisheries operation. It also manages successful ventures including pine forests and social services. In 2006, almost 12,000 people said they were affiliated to Te Whānau-ā-Apanui.

Tūkākī (above left), seen here atop the meeting house at Te Kaha marae, was the son of Apanui Ringamutu and Kahukuramihiata. The meeting house is named after him.

The Mōtū River (above right) was given to Apanui Ringamutu as a young boy. A rock in the river was named after Hinemōtū, a famous Te Whānau-ā-Apanui beauty. She eloped with Tūwharetoa, the ancestor of Ngāti Tūwharetoa, after he visited Te Whānau-ā-Apanui's tribal area.

This map (right) shows the traditional lands of Te Whānau-ā-Apanui.

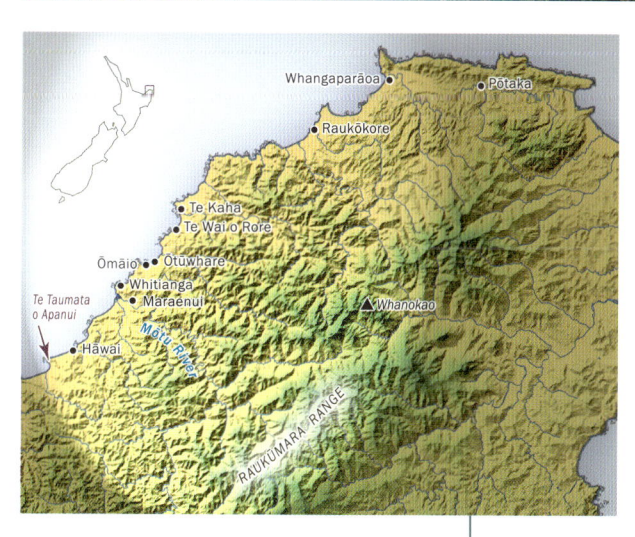

Māori Tribes of New Zealand 55

NGĀTI POROU

When Māui hauled up the North Island from the ocean depths, the first point to emerge was the mountain that Ngāti Porou claim as their sacred icon: Hikurangi.

Subsequent ancestors included Toi, Paikea (the whale rider from Hawaiki), the chief Te Kani-a-Takirau, who refused the offer of kingship, and later, Sir Āpirana Ngata. For Ngāti Porou, independence and unity are as enduring as Mt Hikurangi.

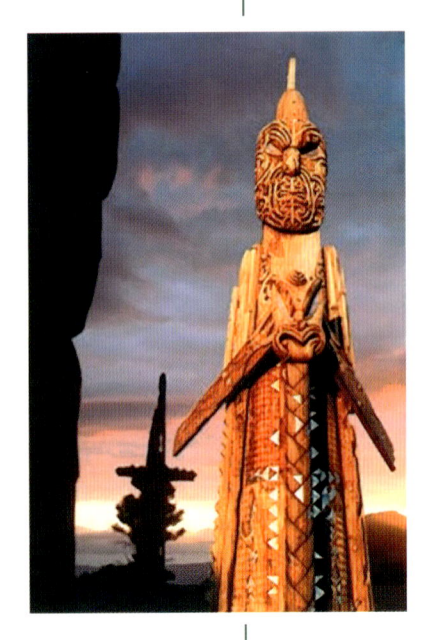

The homeland of Ngāti Porou is the most easterly region in the North Island. It runs north along the coast from Te Toka-a-Taiau at Gisborne, to Pōtikirua, inland from Hicks Bay. Mt Hikurangi is the tribal mountain, and the most important river is Waiapu, an ancient name also found on the Pacific island of Tahiti.

Hikurangi, above, is the sacred mountain of Ngāti Porou. According to tradition, Māui's canoe, Nukutaimemeha, remains stranded on the mountain peak. Hikurangi was acquired by the Crown in the 1870s and became a state forest park. In November 1990 the Crown signed a deed with Te Rūnanga o Ngāti Porou, vesting in them 3,780 hectares which included Hikurangi. Ngāti Porou now manage the land and facilitate public access to the mountain.

These massive sculptures on Mt Hikurangi (left) were commissioned by Te Rūnanga o Ngāti Porou as part of the millennium celebrations. They tell the story of the Ngāti Porou ancestor Māui, who fished the North Island up from the sea. Hikurangi was the first piece of land to emerge, and became the sacred mountain of Ngāti Porou. The Māui whakairo is one of the nine carvings located on Mt Hikurangi, carved by students from Toihoukura under the guidance of Derek Lardelli.

56 Māori Tribes of New Zealand

ANCESTORS

Ngāti Porou take their name from the ancestor Porourangi. His descendants were great warriors who established the tribe's territory in the East Coast and Gisborne regions.

The original ancestor is the godlike Māui, celebrated in Māori tradition and in Ngāti Porou songs and haka. When he fished up the North Island, his canoe *Nukutaimemeha* became stranded on the first peak to appear, Hikurangi.

Other important ancestors are Toi and Paikea. In tradition, Paikea came to New Zealand from Hawaiki on the back of a whale.

Ngāti Porou also share ancestral links with neighbouring tribes such as Ngāti Kahungunu and Te Whānau-ā-Apanui.

CHANGES IN THE 19TH CENTURY

In the 1820s Ngāti Porou people were massacred by Ngāpuhi, armed with European weapons. The arrival of Christianity brought a time of stability. Several chiefs signed the Treaty of Waitangi, and the tribe expanded economically.

In 1865 Ngāti Porou became divided. Some joined the spreading Hauhau movement, which opposed Pākehā taking Māori land. Others fought the Hauhau supporters, using guns supplied by the government.

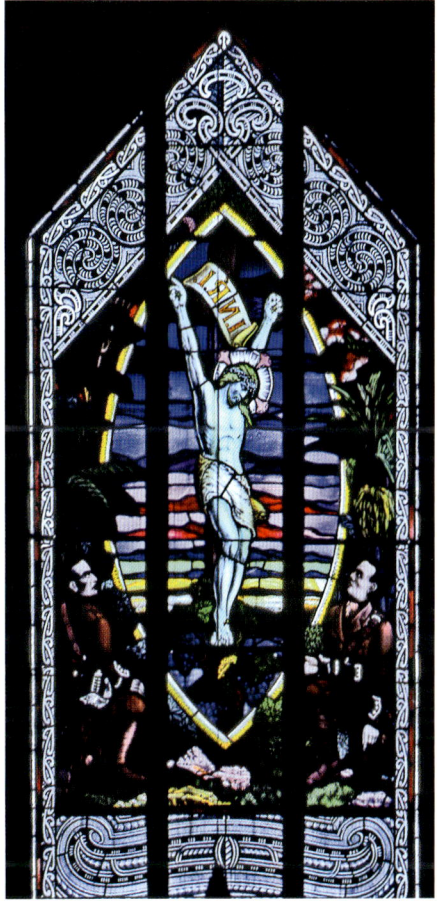

NGĀTI POROU TODAY

The politician Sir Āpirana Ngata was Ngāti Porou's most important leader. From farming to culture to sport, his influence in the first half of the 20th century was immense.

After the Second World War many people joined the drift to the cities, seeking education and a better life.

In 2006 the tribe numbered almost 72,000. Only about one-sixth lived in the tribal territory; most were in Auckland, Wellington and other urban centres.

Christianity was initially welcomed and seen as bringing peace to the Ngāti Porou people, who became strong followers. This window at St Mary's Church in Tikitiki (above) is a memorial to those Ngāti Porou who died in the First World war.

This map (left) shows Ngāti Porou's tribal area as defined under the Te Rūnanga o Ngāti Porou Act 1987, and highlights some of the major natural features and townships of the area.

'Kei te aha country'

Koro Dewes, a Ngāti Porou elder, demonstrated the tribe's particular character at a gathering at Hinerupe marae in 1995. Lining up for the customary greetings, one of the visitors reached Koro and opened with the usual 'Kei te pēhea koe?' (How are you?). Instantly Koro responded, not without a hint of disdain in his tone, 'Eta, you're in "Kei te aha country" now!' 'Kei te aha' is known as the most distinctive greeting of Ngāti Porou.

Māori Tribes of New Zealand 57

TŪRANGANUI-A-KIWA TRIBES

Four tribes dominate the Tūranganui-a-Kiwa (Poverty Bay) area on the East Coast of the North Island.

Their ancestors include Kiwa, who named the region; Pāoa, who explored the hinterland; and Hinehākirirangi, who brought the life-sustaining kūmara (sweet potato) from Hawaiki to New Zealand in her sacred basket.

For centuries Tūranganui-a-Kiwa – the Poverty Bay region on the East Coast of the North Island – has been dominated by four tribes:
- Te Aitanga-a-Māhaki
- Rongowhakaata
- Ngāi Tāmanuhiri
- Te Aitanga-a-Hauiti.

Their people descend from the voyagers of the *Te Ikaroa-a-Rauru*, *Horouta* and *Tākitimu* canoes.

The Tūranganui-a-Kiwa area gets its name from the ancestor Kiwa, who arrived from Hawaiki on the *Tākitimu* canoe. According to one legend, he waited so long for the *Horouta* canoe to arrive that he called its final landing place Tūranganui-a-Kiwa (the long waiting place of Kiwa). Pāoa, captain of the *Horouta*, also gave his name to various places, notably the Wai-o-Pāoa (Waipāoa) River. Another important ancestor was Hinehākirirangi, who brought kūmara (sweet potato) from Hawaiki in her sacred basket. Eventually a descendant of the three ancestors Kiwa, Pāoa and Hinehākirirangi emerged as a leader – his name was Ruapani.

This prominent headland, 27 km south of Gisborne, is a significant place for Tūranganui-a-Kiwa tribes. Its name, Te Kurī-a-Pāoa, means 'the dog of Pāoa'. Pāoa was the captain of the Horouta canoe. Later, Captain James Cook named it Young Nick's Head, in honour of the cabin boy who first sighted land from the Endeavour. In 2003 there was an outcry when an American purchased the headland. Subsequently, the cliffs, a pā site and the peak were placed in public ownership.

Te Kooti's personal battle flag was known as Te Wepu (the whip). Te Kooti captured it from Ngāti Kahungunu in 1868, and in 1875 he said, 'The whip will shortly be applied to the whole land.' The flag was very large, measuring 16 metres in length. The crescent moon is a portent of the new world, and the cross is the fighting cross of the Archangel Michael. The mountain represents New Zealand and the bleeding heart the suffering of the Māori people.

EUROPEAN ARRIVALS

People from Tūranganui-a-Kiwa met Captain James Cook and his crew when they arrived on the *Endeavour* in 1769. In the 1800s more Europeans – whalers, traders, missionaries and then settlers – came to the region. Tūranganui-a-Kiwa tribes did not join in the wars between Māori and the government in the early 1860s. But when the government began to confiscate their land, the tribes' attitude changed. They realised the threat to Māori society.

Prophets of the Hauhau (Pai Mārire) faith, which was opposed by the government, came to Poverty Bay in 1865. Many people decided to join their religion. After clashes between Hauhau supporters and government forces, Māori prisoners were sent to the Chatham Islands. One Rongowhakaata man, Te Kooti, led a mass escape and an attack on Poverty Bay, and became an important leader and prophet. Government forces pursued him into Te Urewera, but he avoided being captured, and became the founder of the Ringatū religion.

LAND DEVELOPMENT

In the later 19th century, leaders of Tūranganui-a-Kiwa promoted the idea of setting up trusts to keep and look after Māori land. In the 20th century the tribes worked to develop their land.

THE TŪRANGANUI-A-KIWA TRIBES TODAY

Many from Tūranganui-a-Kiwa fought in the world wars. Others were active in helping returned soldiers settle back into society. Following the Second World War, the Māori Women's Welfare League established many branches in the area. The main community organisation is now Te Rūnanga o Tūranganui a Kiwa, which provides social, education, land management and health services. In the 2006 census, more than 12,000 people said they were descended from Tūranganui-a-Kiwa tribes.

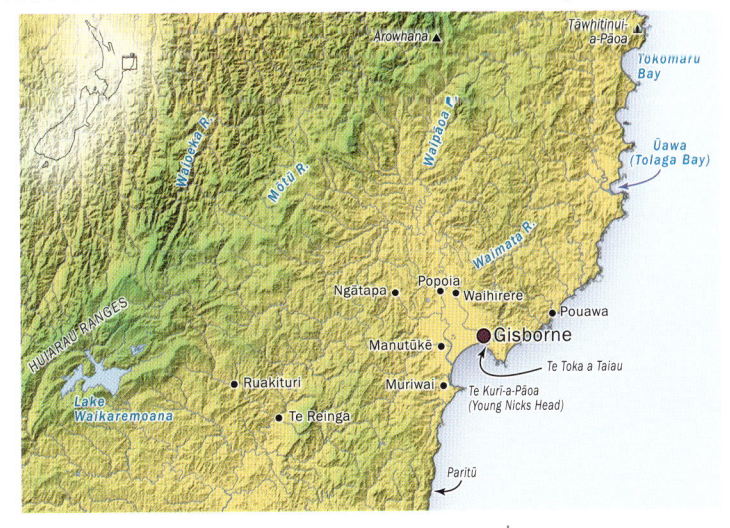

This map shows the traditional area occupied by the tribes of Tūranganui-a-Kiwa.

Māori Tribes of New Zealand

NGĀTI RONGOMAIWAHINE

> Rongomaiwahine was a woman of very great status, and her descendants are Ngāti Rongomaiwahine. Because of the mana of their ancestor, Ngāti Rongomaiwahine hold firmly to their identity.
>
> At Māhia Peninsula, on the eastern coast of New Zealand, Ngāti Rongomaiwahine have extensive traditional fishing grounds. The area has many sacred sites which reflect the significance of whales to the tribe, including a whale-shaped hill, Te Ara-a-Paikea.

Rongomaiwahine was the ancestor of the people of the Māhia Peninsula. She was married to the carver Tamatakutai, but another man, Kahungunu, wanted to have Rongomaiwahine for himself. Tamatakutai was drowned in the crashing surf off the peninsula, and eventually Rongomaiwahine married Kahungunu, the ancestor of Ngāti Kahungunu. They had five children.

RESOURCES FROM SEA AND LAND

Before the arrival of Europeans, the people of Ngāti Rongomaiwahine were able to live from the fruits of the sea and land. Food sources around the peninsula included abundant shellfish, seaweed, eels and whitebait. In the 1830s and 1840s there were whaling stations at Māhia Peninsula. After the stations closed, the people of Ngāti Rongomaiwahine continued to hunt for whales. Inland, the bush provided food and timber resources. Now sheep and cattle are grazed on farmed land. Te Whānau o Rongomaiwahine Trust has been established to ensure the resources of the peninsula are used for the benefit of its people.

This plaque at Coronation Reserve, Whangawehi, on Māhia Peninsula, marks a hollow rock that was used as a baptismal font in 1842. The Anglican missionary William Williams baptised 245 people there.

SIGNIFICANT PLACES

Some features of Māhia Peninsula are of great ancestral significance. One of the area's most sacred sites is a whale-shaped hill called Te Ara-a-Paikea.

On the western side of the peninsula, the wind rushing through a hole in the summit of another hill, Taupiri, mimics the sound of whale song. Other areas are rich in local history and legend. The pool known as Te Wai Whakaata-a-Tūtāmure is where Tūtāmure looked at his reflection and decided that his younger brother was more handsome, and the more fitting husband for Rongomaiwahine's daughter, Tauheikurī.

NGĀTI RONGOWMAIWAHINE TODAY

In the 2006 census, more than 4,000 people said they were affiliated with Ngāti Rongomaiwahine.

Mokotahi was once the site of Tirotirokauika pā. This was the second dwelling place of Ruawharo, the priest of the Tākitimu canoe.

This map shows Māhia Peninsula, which is the tribal area of Ngāti Rongomaiwahine.

Karaka tree

It is said that the karaka (*Corynocarpus laevigatus*) was brought to New Zealand by the people of the *Kurahaupō* canoe, which landed at Tawapata on Māhia Peninsula. The berry of the karaka tree was greatly valued as a food by Māori. However, its seed is poisonous and could not be safely eaten without a great deal of preparation to remove the poison.

Rongomaiwahine is the central figure in this lintel, at Kahungunu marae in Nūhaka.

Māori Tribes of New Zealand 61

NGĀTI KAHUNGUNU

Handsome and hard-working, the influential leader Kahungunu supervised building, irrigation, carving and canoe-making. During his life he married nine women, and his courtship of the beautiful Rongomaiwahine at Māhia Peninsula is legendary.

Kahungunu's many descendants – the people of Ngāti Kahungunu – also formed strategic marriages, creating a network of alliances from Gisborne to the Wairarapa.

Two Central Hawke's Bay Council workers, above, Dennis Goodley and David Blackledge, stand in front of a sign they have just fixed which marks the world's longest place name. The place is on Wimbledon Road, Pōrangahau, and the name means 'The place where the great explorer Tamatea [Kahungunu's father], the man with the big knees, who slid, climbed and swallowed mountains, known as landeater, played the flute to his loved one'.

Ngāti Kahungunu are New Zealand's third largest tribal group. Stretching down the North Island from the Māhia Peninsula to Cape Palliser, their territory is divided into three districts: Wairoa, Heretaunga and Wairarapa.

ANCESTORS

The tribe originates from the *Tākitimu* canoe, sailed from Hawaiki by Tamatea Arikinui. His son Rongokako married Muriwhenua and they had a son, the great explorer Tamatea Ure Haea.

At Kaitāia, Tamatea Ure Haea's son Kahungunu was born. An energetic and talented leader, Kahungunu built villages and irrigated the land. Travelling south, he fathered many children, whose descendants eventually became known as Ngāti Kahungunu. At Māhia, Kahungunu married high-born Rongomaiwahine, having cleverly disposed of her husband. From this famous love match came a line of prominent figures in the tribe's history.

Māori Tribes of New Zealand

EUROPEAN CONTACT

After Pākehā arrived, some tribes acquired muskets. Under gunfire attack from northern tribes, many Ngāti Kahungunu people from Napier escaped to Māhia.

Whaling stations were set up on tribal land in the 1830s, and Ngāti Kahungunu began farming and market gardening. Some of the tribe's chiefs signed the Treaty of Waitangi in 1840, but European settlers soon acquired a massive amount of their ancestral land.

Pāpāwai village in the Wairarapa became a centre for teaching tribal history, and the site of the Māori parliament. The wealthy political leader Tamahau Mahupuku held grand gatherings there, and would travel to town accompanied by a brass band.

NGĀTI KAHUNGUNU TODAY

In 2006 there were around 59,000 people in the tribe, and 86 marae administered by Ngāti Kahungunu Iwi Incorporated. Cultural ventures included Radio Kahungunu and the internationally successful Māori Dance Theatre.

This map shows the three main Ngāti Kahungunu areas within the tribal boundaries. The three divisions are Ngāti Kahungunu ki Te Wairoa, Ngāti Kahungunu ki Heretaunga and Ngāti Kahungunu ki Te Wairarapa. The many lakes and rivers, and harbours such as Hawke Bay (Te Matau-a-Māui), were important as highways and a source of food.

Leftovers for the enemy

When Ngāpuhi, armed with muskets, came to raid the Wairoa district the people fled to their formidable pā high above Mōrere, south-east of Nūhaka. Ngāpuhi laid siege, but the pā's food stores were plentiful, and soon it was the attackers who were starving. The defenders taunted Ngāpuhi by throwing scraps of food to them – hence the name Moumoukai (wasteful of food). Eventually, Ngāpuhi lifted the siege. Pōmare of Ngāpuhi asked that a couple name their child after him. So it was that the name Pōmare came to be a Nūhaka family name.

One of the most famous New Zealand love stories began on the Māhia Peninsula. It was here, at Nukutaurua, far left, that Kahungunu met and married Rongomaiwahine.

This carving in Ngāti Kahungunu style, left, now held in the Museum of New Zealand Te Papa Tongarewa, is thought to depict the ancestor Kahungunu, who was renowned for his leadership and practical skills.

TE ĀTI AWA OF TARANAKI

According to legend, the people of Te Āti Awa have both mortal and immortal origins. They are descended from Awanuiarangi, the son of a woman, Rongoueroa, and a spirit descended from the sky, Tamarau-te-heketanga-a-rangi.

In 1860 a dramatic event had a huge impact on Te Āti Awa. When the tribe's chief, Wiremu Kīngi Te Rangitāke, refused to vacate his home after it had been sold to Europeans, the British fired the shots that were to begin the New Zealand wars.

The traditional lands of Te Āti Awa of Taranaki stretch from the coast north of New Plymouth, to Mt Taranaki (Mt Egmont), and to the Matemateaonga ranges in the south.

TE ĀTI AWA ORIGINS

Te Āti Awa is one of several Awa tribes, all descended from Awanuiarangi. He was the son of a mortal woman, Rongoueroa, and a sky spirit, Tamarau-te-heke-tanga-a-rangi.

The Awa tribes – which include Ngāti Awa in the Bay of Plenty – separated in 1820 and are now independent groups with their own authority. The individual identity of Te Āti Awa in Taranaki is expressed in their association with the *Tokomaru* canoe.

EUROPEANS ARRIVE

The arrival of European settlers in Taranaki caused upheavals for Te Āti Awa. Having come with the express purpose of farming, New Zealand Company immigrants snapped up the fertile Te Āti Awa land. This disrupted both the Taranaki area and the tribe itself – some of whom wanted to sell land to settlers, while others opposed land sales. Even though the tribe were divided, their chief Wiremu Kīngi Te Rangitāke managed to establish a thriving economy by selling crops to the new settlers. However, when settlers bought the tribe's land, Kīngi refused to leave. The British fired at him, and in 1860 the New Zealand wars broke out.

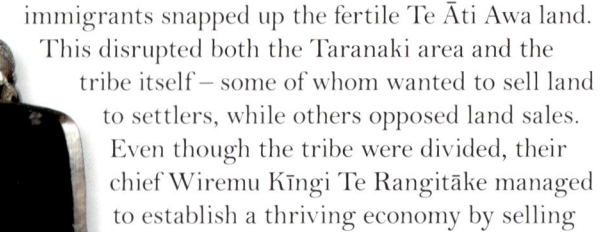

After a year of fighting, Māori were defeated and their land was confiscated as a punishment for their rebellion. The loss of land was socially, culturally and politically debilitating for Te Āti Awa. Their 90 sub-tribes were reduced to the six of today.

This tauihu (bow figurehead) was gifted to the Duke of Edinburgh during his visit to New Zealand in 1869. It was carved by Wiremu Kīngi Te Rangitāke, the paramount Te Āti Awa chief, who led the return of his people from the Waikanae–Wellington area to Taranaki in 1848. He recognised that traditional lands were under threat from the growing number of settlers and opposed the sale of land.

Mt Taranaki is the most significant mountain for Te Āti Awa, as for some other Taranaki tribes. The mountain is on the south-east corner of the tribe's traditional lands.

TE ĀTI AWA TODAY

Throughout the early 20th century Te Āti Awa land was still being sold off, despite calls for settlement. In 1996 the Waitangi Tribunal acknowledged past breaches of the Treaty of Waitangi, and negotiations for compensation began. In the 2006 census, 12,852 people claimed descent from Te Āti Awa of Taranaki.

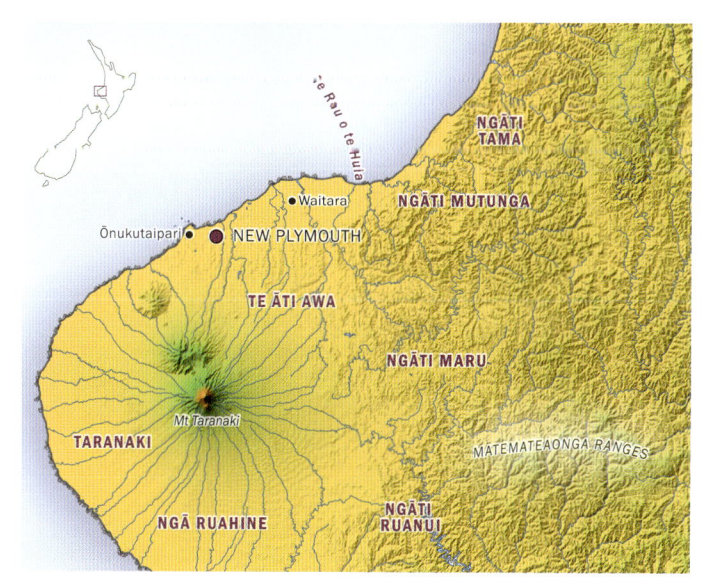

This map shows the traditional lands of Te Āti Awa of Taranaki. On the coast, the western boundary is Ōnukutaipari, near New Plymouth, and the northern boundary is Te Rau o te Huia, near Motunui. The inland boundaries, some of which are disputed by neighbouring tribes, stretch from the north-eastern slopes of Mt Taranaki inland to the Matemateaonga Ranges.

Māori Tribes of New Zealand   65

TARANAKI

The mountains of the Kaitake Range, Pouākai Range and Mt Taranaki (Mt Egmont) dominate the territory and history of the Taranaki tribe. They symbolise the peaceful endurance of a people who have survived invasion and confiscation of their land, and are now looking to the future.

Mt Taranaki dominates the Taranaki tribal area. The mountains are central to the identity of the tribe: the original ancestors were called Te Kāhui Maunga – the people of the mountains.

The area of the Taranaki tribe covers the west cape of the North Island. It stretches from Ōnukutaipari in the north to the Ōuri River in the south, and includes Mt Taranaki (Mt Egmont).

The earliest ancestors of the Taranaki people were called Te Kāhui Maunga – the people of the mountains. Mt Taranaki was named after Rua Taranaki, the first in a line of chiefs. The Taranaki tribe emerged when arrivals from the *Kurahaupō* canoe intermarried with the people of the mountains.

WAR WITH OTHER TRIBES AND EUROPEANS

The Taranaki tribe's close relationship with neighbouring tribes was constantly changing. This was because of regular raids by Waikato tribes from the late 1700s, and the arrival of other northern tribes armed with muskets in the early 1800s. Some other tribes moved south, changing the balance of power in the region.

There was further upheaval when European settlers arrived in New Zealand after 1840. Their demand for land suitable for farming put pressure on all Taranaki tribes to sell. The tribes refused, and war broke out between Māori and the government in 1860. Many villages in the Taranaki region were destroyed. Land was confiscated by the government and sold for settlement.

How Taranaki got its name
Tradition holds that the chief Tahurangi climbed the peak and lit a ceremonial fire, which caused an alpine cloud to descend. In this rite the name of the ancestor Rua Taranaki was conferred on the mountain. The people of the Taranaki tribe have a saying:

The fire of Tahurangi brings forth the alpine cloud.
It stands elevated.
And falls in the dawn and in the evenings.

THE HAUHAU FAITH

In 1862 Te Ua Haumēne of the Taranaki tribe founded a new religion, called Hauhau (also known as Pai Mārire, meaning 'goodness and peace'). The faith taught that Māori people would eventually get back their land. It spread rapidly among Māori, and was seen as a threat by Europeans. Fighting broke out between Hauhau followers and government forces.

PARIHAKA AND PEACEFUL PROTEST

In the mid-1860s the village of Parihaka was the centre of a movement which encouraged non-violent resistance to the confiscation of land. Its followers prevented surveys, and ploughed and fenced land that was occupied by European settlers. Many of the protesters were arrested and held without trial, but the protests continued. Finally, government troops marched on Parihaka in 1881, arresting and driving away its inhabitants. Some were imprisoned without trial until the late 1890s.

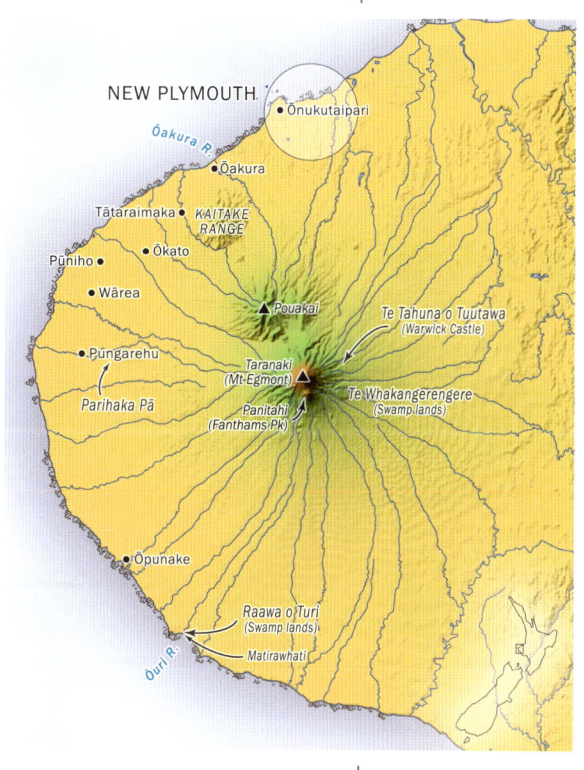

This map shows the major landmarks in the traditional area of the Taranaki tribe. Ōnukutaipari marks the northern boundary, while the Ōuri River forms the southern boundary. The territory includes Mt Taranaki (Egmont).

THE TARANAKI TRIBE TODAY

Today there is a new interest in the tribe's traditional knowledge and culture, and the story of Parihaka continues to inspire art, poetry and song. More than 5,300 people said they were descended from the Taranaki tribe in 2006.

Before flax could be woven, the outer green layer was removed and the inner fibres were soaked and pounded until soft. This patu muka (flax pounder), above, was a tool used in the process. Flax was an important item in the Māori economy, and the skills associated with its preparation were highly prized. During the early 19th century, aggressive northern tribes captured Taranaki slaves skilled in flax work. The labour of these slaves earned money so their captors could buy muskets for further intertribal warfare.

Ralph Hotere's 1972 painting 'Comet over Mt Egmont', right, was inspired by an extraordinary and portentous photograph taken in 1882, which showed a comet in the sky over Mt Taranaki, with Parihaka village in the foreground.

Māori Tribes of New Zealand 67

NGĀTI RUANUI

Ngāti Ruanui's early identity was forged in battle. The tribe's ancestor, Turi, left the Pacific island of Rangiātea to escape a blood feud. With his people, he endured many trials at sea before arriving and settling in south Taranaki. Generations later, the people of Ngāti Ruanui were besieged by warring tribes, as well as by British soldiers in the wars of the 1860s.

The Ngāti Ruanui ancestor Turi fled the island of Rangiātea to save his life. In a canoe laden with plants and animals, Turi and his people sailed across the Pacific. After many tribulations they arrived in New Zealand. They established their tribal area in south Taranaki, between the Whenuakura River and the Ōeo Stream, where they lived for many generations.

INTERTRIBAL WARS

Ngāti Ruanui were invaded by neighbouring tribes during the early 1800s. Muskets wreaked havoc, and many members of Ngāti Ruanui lost their lives or were taken as slaves.

To bring peace, the Ngāti Hao chief Patuone arranged marriages between Ngāti Ruanui and people of his tribe. But restful times were short-lived and inter-tribal war did not stop until the 1830s. By this time Ngāti Ruanui had suffered serious losses of people, and many were driven from their land.

This bus, from Ngāti Ruanui's Taiporohēnui marae in Hāwera, features an image of Mt Taranaki on the back and the name of the Aotea canoe above its door. Hāmua and Hapōtiki, painted on the side of the bus, are Ngāti Ruanui sub-tribes.

68 Māori Tribes of New Zealand

Mt Taranaki is regarded as wāhi tapu (a sacred area) by all tribes in the province of Taranaki. Here, it is viewed from the famous Ngāti Tūpaea pā of Turuturumōkai, where Tītokowaru began his war against European soldiers in 1868.

CONFLICT OVER LAND

Ngāti Ruanui were quick to recover, adapting readily to European agriculture and education. But they were also wary of European influences, preferring to run their own schools for political reasons.

However, the wars of the 1860s saw Ngāti Ruanui disadvantaged again. They joined forces with Te Āti Awa to fight against the British Crown and protect their land. The military leader Tītokowaru played an important role in the conflict. In 1868 he attacked an outpost and later successfully defended his pā, Te Ngutu-o-te-manu. But the government eventually gained control of south Taranaki.

Ngāti Ruanui became the main tribe of south Taranaki. This map shows their tribal area.

NGĀTI RUANUI TODAY

These days Ngāti Ruanui live all over New Zealand, and the world. Their recent success in winning compensation for the land taken from them in the 1860s means that funds and resources have been channelled back into the tribe for the benefit of all its members. More than 7,000 people claimed affiliation with Ngāti Ruanui in the 2006 census; most lived outside Taranaki.

Guide Sophia

About 1829 Kōtiro Hinerangi of Ngāti Ruanui was taken to Ngāpuhi by a raiding party as a slave for Hōne Heke. However, she soon married a Scot, Alexander Grey. Their daughter Te Paea (Mary Sophia Grey) was born about 1832. She later became famous as the main guide to the Pink and White Terraces at Lake Rotomahana before they were destroyed by the Tarawera eruption in 1886. A few days before the eruption Sophia had seen a phantom canoe on the lake, which she interpreted as a bad omen. After the destruction Sophia moved to Rotorua, where she was a guide at Whakarewarewa until she died in 1911.

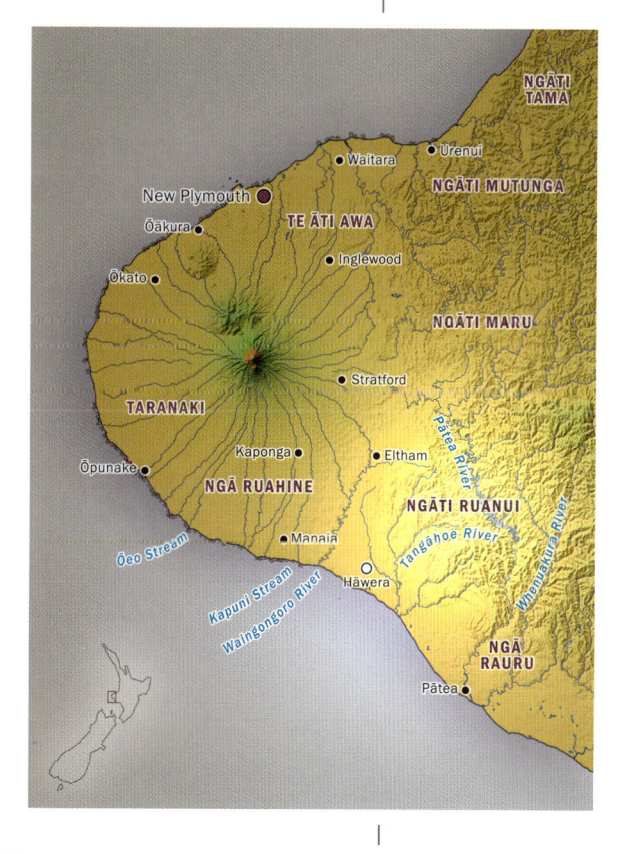

Māori Tribes of New Zealand 69

NGĀ RAURU KĪTAHI

Ngā Rauru Kītahi take their name from the ancestor Rauru. With a reputation as a warrior and man of his word, he was called Rauru Kītahi – 'Rauru of the one word'.

It is a great compliment to be described as like Rauru – true to your word.

The traditional lands of the south Taranaki tribe Ngā Rauru Kītahi extend between the Wanganui and Pātea rivers. Ngā Rauru descend from an early tribe called Te Kāhui Rere (the flying people), who lived around Waitōtara. Members of Te Kāhui Rere intermarried with the people who arrived in south Taranaki aboard the *Aotea* canoe.

The tribe is named after an important ancestor, Rauru Kītahi (Rauru of the one word). A grandson of the early Polynesian explorer Toitehuatahi, Rauru was born at Whakatāne and travelled extensively. He ended his days with the people of south Taranaki, who named themselves in his honour.

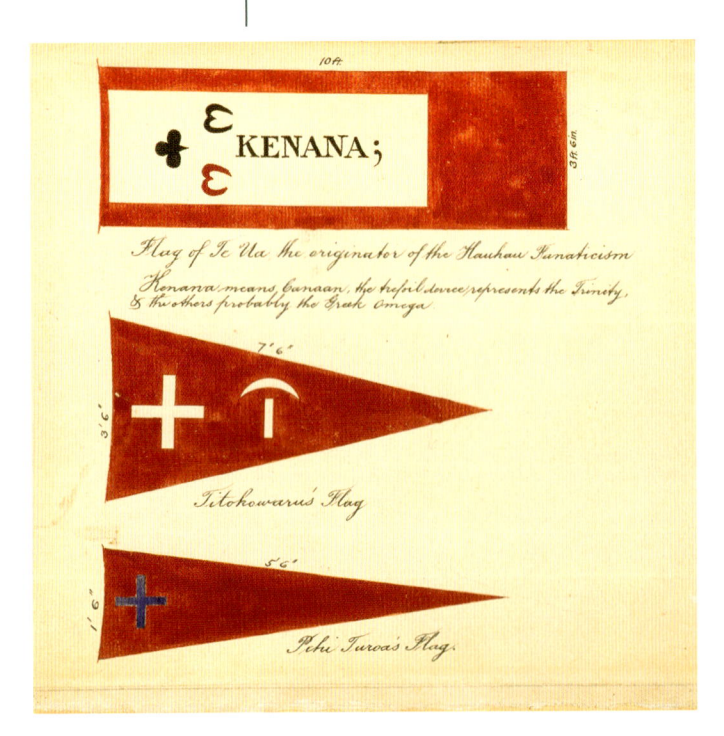

LAND AND AUTHORITY

From the early 19th century Ngāti Toa and other Taranaki peoples moved south into Ngā Rauru territory in search of new land and resources. When Europeans settled in the area after 1840, some of the tribe were willing to sell land to the government, but others objected. The refusal to sell led to war between the government and Māori in the 1860s. A large amount of Taranaki land was taken by the government, including over 60,700 hectares of Ngā Rauru territory, and some people were put in prison. Later, Ngā Rauru people took part in the peaceful passive resistance protests at Parihaka in 1881, and some were imprisoned by the government.

The Pai Mārire (Hauhau) faith was a Māori resistance movement which gained many followers, including some members of Ngā Rauru, during the wars of the 1860s in Taranaki. The illustration shows from top to bottom, the personal standards of Pai Mārire leaders Te Ua Haumēne, Tītokowaru, and Te Peehi Tūroa.

MĀORI RELIGIOUS AND POLITICAL MOVEMENTS

Some members of Ngā Rauru joined new Māori religious and political movements. These included Pai Mārire (Hauhau), the Rātana Church and Te Māramatanga (enlightenment).

This map shows the area traditionally occupied by Ngā Rauru, stretching between the Whanganui and Pātea rivers.

NGĀ RAURU KĪTAHI TODAY

Moves to compensate Ngā Rauru for land confiscation and the loss of their livelihood began in the 1880s, but were ineffective. It was not until 2003 that the tribe signed a settlement with the government that gave them financial and other compensation, and an apology.

In 2006 the tribe had more than 4,000 members, belonging to 14 sub-tribes. The tribal authority organises commercial ventures, such as making traditional herbal remedies. It is also working to revitalise Ngā Raurutanga – the values, customs and beliefs that are unique to Ngā Rauru.

Rongoueroa was the mother of Rauru Kītahi, the ancestor from whom the tribe Ngā Rauru Kītahi take their name. She was also the mother of Awainuiarangi, the ancestor of the Te Āti Awa people.

The Aotea *canoe landed close to the Pātea River mouth. Later Ngā Rauru built settlements along the river.*

Māori Tribes of New Zealand 71

WHANGANUI TRIBES

'Ko au te awa. Ko te awa ko au.'
'I am the river. The river is me.'

The tribes of Whanganui take their name, their spirit and their strength from the great river which flows from the mountains of the central North Island to the sea.

For centuries the people have travelled the Whanganui River by canoe, caught eels in it, built villages on its banks, and fought over it.

The peoples of the Whanganui River are collectively called Ngāti Hau. The ancestors associated with the river include:

KUPE
The renowned explorer paddled to a place where one of his men, Arapāoa, drowned swimming across the flooded river. Kupe named the spot Kauarapāoa.

HAUNUI-A-PĀPĀRANGI
According to some traditions, Haunui-a-Pāpārangi gave his name to the people of the river, Ngāti Hau. He arrived with Turi, captain of the *Aotea* canoe.

HAUPIPI
Haupipi also arrived with Turi. Some believe that Ngāti Hau are named after him.

TAMATEA-PŌKAI-WHENUA
This famous explorer sent a servant ashore to find flax for a topknot (pūtiki). The place came to be called Pūtiki, and is today a village across the river from Whanganui.

One great explorer of the river was Tamatea-pōkaiwhenua, captain of the Tākitimu canoe. His name is commemorated in a remarkable cave on the upper reaches of the river. This is a view from inside the cave.

THE PLAITED ROPE

The unity of the Whanganui River peoples is expressed in a famous saying, 'te taura whiri a Hinengākau' (the plaited rope of Hinengākau). This refers to the three closely connected groups of the river, and before them to the ancestor Tamakehu's three children: Hinengākau of the upper river, Tama Ūpoko of the middle, and Tūpoho of the lower Whanganui.

WAR

Whanganui tribes were attacked by tribes from the north in the 1820s. Then Europeans settled in Whanganui town in 1840. The people of the lower Whanganui River began to trade with the town, and many were converted to Christianity. Their upper river cousins became involved in a new religion called Pai Mārire or Hauhau, which opposed European settlement. The two groups fought, and the most tragic event was a battle on a small island, Moutoa, in the middle of the river, in 1864. But the two groups joined together again in 1869 to fight against the guerrilla leader Te Kooti, in the upper river area.

WHANGANUI TRIBES TODAY

Riverboats brought tourism to the river and upset traditional practices such as harvesting eels. For over a century the Whanganui tribes fought for their rights to the river, and in 1995 they occupied Pākaitore (Moutoa Gardens) for 79 days to defend their claims.

About 12,300 people were affiliated with the Whanganui tribes in 2006.

From 1819 Ngāpuhi swept through the Whanganui region. In one incident Tūwhare of Ngāpuhi led a raiding party against Te Hā Mārama and his people. Tūwhare was wounded but not killed, and he taunted Te Hā by saying that his hand was 'he ringa mahi kai' – the hand of a food provider. However, Te Hā replied that he had spared Tūwhare so that he could tell others of Te Hā's fierceness. This taiaha, below, then took on the name 'Te ringa mahi kai'.

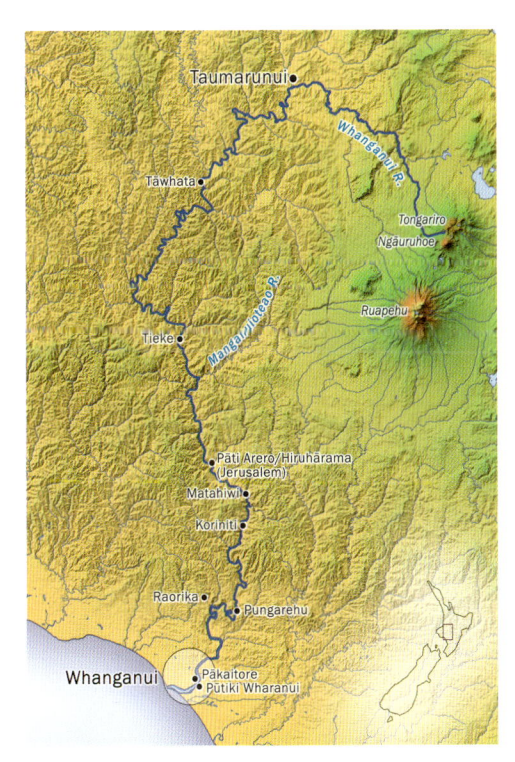

This map shows the full length of the Whanganui River, which flows from Mt Tongariro to the sea. Some of the major pā sites on the river are also marked.

NGĀTI APA

> The people of Ngāti Apa live in the Rangitīkei region in the North Island. In the 19th century the tribe became known for its prophets and visionaries, who set up enduring Māori faiths, notably the Māramatanga movement and the Rātana Church.

The carved Ngāti Apa meeting house Rangitahuahua, above, is situated at Whangaehu marae.

The Whanganui River marks the north, and the Manawatū River the south of Ngāti Apa's territory. Their traditional lands lie between the Mangawhero, Whangaehu, Turakina and Rangitīkei rivers.

Ngāti Apa trace their ancestry to Ruatea, captain of the *Kurahaupō* canoe. They take their name from Ruatea's son, Apa-hāpai-taketake (Apa), who lived near Pūtauaki (Mt Edgecumbe) in the Bay of Plenty.

MIGRATIONS AND EUROPEAN SETTLEMENT

Over time, some of Apa's descendants moved south to the Rangitīkei area. Others migrated even further south, some reaching the northern part of the South Island. Those who went to Rangitīkei intermarried with the Ngā Wairiki people, and eventually became known as Ngāti Apa.

Ngāti Apa were initially receptive to Europeans. They signed the Treaty of Waitangi in 1840 and welcomed missionaries working in the Whanganui and Rangitīkei areas. In 1849 the tribe sold land to the government, expecting trade and other benefits. However, these benefits did not eventuate. European farming destroyed traditional food-gathering sites. Eventually Ngāti Apa lost much of their land and were reduced to poverty.

RELIGION AND POLITICS

Facing so many difficulties, Ngāti Apa started several new religious movements. The prophet Mere Rikiriki inspired some important religious leaders, including Hōri Ēnoka (Mareikura), founder of the Māramatanga movement, and Tahupōtiki Wiremu Rātana, who established the Rātana Church.

NGĀTI APA TODAY

Today the tribe is represented by Te Rūnanga o Ngāti Apa. This organisation researches tribal land claims made to the Waitangi Tribunal, and organises health education. Restoring the tribe's unity and prestige remains a central aim. In 2006, 4,152 people claimed descent from Ngāti Apa.

The traditional tribal area of Ngāti Apa stretches between the Whanganui and Manawatū rivers, and includes the Mangawhero, Whangaehu, Turakina and Rangitīkei rivers.

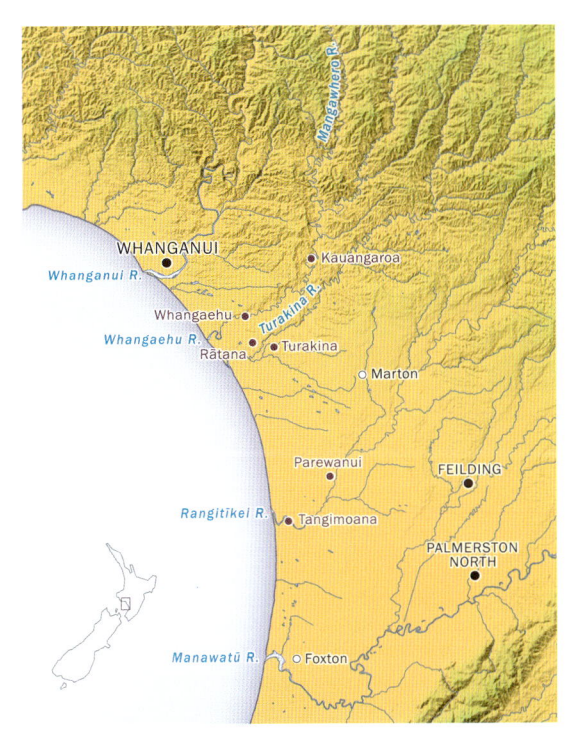

The Rangitīkei River is at the heart of Ngāti Apa's traditional lands. Many significant tribal events have taken place on its banks.

Māori Tribes of New Zealand 75

RANGITĀNE

The Rangitāne tribe are descended from Whātonga, who came to New Zealand from Hawaiki as a captain of the *Kurahaupō* canoe.

As testament to early tribal expansion, their marae can still be found throughout the country.

The people of Rangitāne are descendants of Whātonga, captain of the *Kurahaupō* canoe. The canoe arrived at Māhia Peninsula on the East Coast of the North Island. The tribe take their name from Whātonga's grandson, Rangitāne (also known as Tānenui-a-rangi).

At first Rangitāne lived in the Heretaunga (Hastings) area. Later, they travelled south and occupied Tāmakinui-a-Rua (present-day Dannevirke), Wairarapa, Te Whanganui-a-Tara (Wellington), and Wairau in the South Island. They also moved west to Manawatū and Horowhenua, the tribe's main centres today.

CHANGES AND CHALLENGES

In the 19th century northern tribes moved into Rangitāne's western territories, and there were many battles. European settlers later took possession of much of the tribe's land in the Manawatū and Dannevirke areas. Although Rangitāne turned to farming in the 20th century, many had to sell up and move to the towns.

The Manawatū Gorge links the western area of Rangitāne settlement, around Palmerston North, with the eastern settlement near Dannevirke.

> **Trailblazing families**
>
> Tipi Rōpiha was the first Māori to lead a government department, as under-secretary for Māori Affairs from 1948 to 1957. His daughter, Rina Moore, was the first Māori woman to graduate as a medical doctor, in 1949. Lui Paewai was a member of the 1924 'Invincible' All Blacks. His nephew Manahi Paewai played rugby for the New Zealand Māoris in 1950–51 and was also a doctor. Eddie Taihākurei Durie, grandson of John Mason Durie, was the first Māori to be appointed a judge of the Māori Land Court in 1974, and of the High Court in 1998.

LEADERS

Rangitāne had strong leaders who helped the tribe adjust to change in the 19th century. They encouraged the people to work with Pākehā. In the 20th century Rangitāne leaders were involved in local and national politics.

Te Rau o Te Aroha Maori Battalion Hall in Palmerston North, designed by John Scott and opened in 1964, blends Māori and Pākehā design elements.

RANGITĀNE TODAY

Te Rūnanganui o Rangitāne was founded in 1988 as a forum for the various tribal committees to discuss national tribal matters. There are seven Rangitāne marae, and some new meeting houses have been built. Almost 4,500 people said they were affiliated to Rangitāne in 2006.

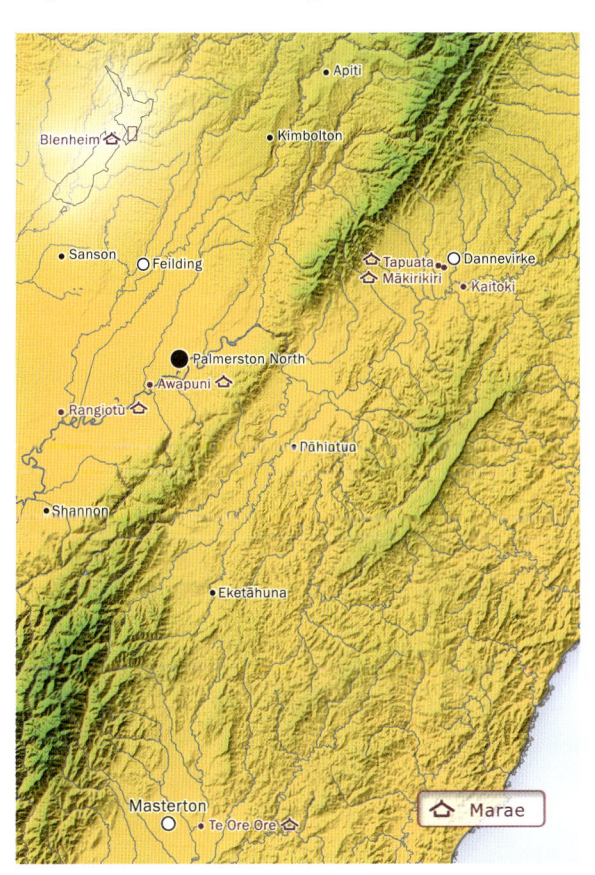

Rangitāne marae are located in the Manawatū, Dannevirke, Wairarapa and Blenheim districts. The scattered nature of these marae reflects the wide area settled by the tribe.

Rangitāne, also known as Rangitānenui, Tānenui-a-rangi and Rangitānenui-a-rangi, was the ancestor from whom the Rangitāne tribe took its name.

Māori Tribes of New Zealand 77

MUAŪPOKO

The Muaūpoko people – formerly known as Ngāi Tara – were named because they lived at the ūpoko (head) of Te Ika-a-Māui – the fish of Māui, or the North Island. Over time, they lost much of their land.

Today, the tribe is working to restore Lake Horowhenua and revive their culture.

The people of Muaūpoko were originally called Ngāi Tara, after their ancestor Tara. His parents, who lived in Hawke's Bay, were Whātonga, chief of the *Kurahaupō* canoe, and Hotuwaipara. Just before she gave birth, Hotuwaipara accidentally pricked her finger with the tara (spine) of a fish, so her son was named Tara.

Later the family moved to the Wellington region. Tara's name was given to the harbour there, which became known as Te Whanganui-a-Tara (the great harbour of Tara). The Ngāi Tara people eventually took the name Muaūpoko, to indicate that they lived at the head (ūpoko) of Te Ika-a-Māui – the legendary fish of Māui, or the North Island.

MUAŪPOKO TERRITORY

At first Ngāi Tara lived around Wellington Harbour and on the Kapiti coast, sharing the land with other tribes. But from the 1820s Ngāti Toa, Te Āti Awa and other tribes moved in from the north. After battling with Ngāti Toa, Muaūpoko were forced to move to Horowhenua and Manawatū.

The beautiful Lake Papaitonga is famous in Muaūpoko history. It was there in the 1820s that the tribe attacked Ngāti Toa and killed two children of the chief Te Rauparaha, to avenge the murder, by Ngāti Toa, of a Muaūpoko woman.

LOSS OF LAND

In 1839 the Te Āti Awa chiefs sold land around Wellington Harbour to the New Zealand Company, who wanted it for the first European settlers. Although Muaūpoko also had interests in the land, they were not consulted. Other tribes challenged Muaūpoko over their land at Horowhenua, and they lost even more. When the settlers arrived, the tribe's wealth and power dwindled further. Farming and forest clearing spoilt the water and reduced the numbers of fish in Lake Horowhenua.

MUAŪPOKO TODAY

The Muaūpoko Tribal Authority, based at Levin in the Horowhenua region, provides health and welfare services. It is also reviving the traditions, history and culture of the tribe. Muaūpoko have formed the Lake Horowhenua Trust, which is working to improve the lake's water quality and fill it with fish, and to restore the bush on the lake's edges. In the 2006 census, 2,499 people claimed Muaūpoko descent.

Fish's head

The name Muaūpoko comes from mua (in front of) and ūpoko (the head). This refers to the shape of the North Island, which tradition holds is the fish landed by Māui. Its head forms the Wellington region, which is the territory of the Muaūpoko people.

Marokopa Wiremu-Matakātea, above, the nursery manager and a trustee for the Lake Horowhenua Trust, checks on the progress of seedlings planted around the lake, which is a traditional food-gathering site for Muaūpoko. The lake and its surrounds became polluted because of vegetation clearance and farming activities, and as a consequence the fish and bird populations declined. Now Muaūpoko are working through the trust to restore the lake environment and replenish its fisheries.

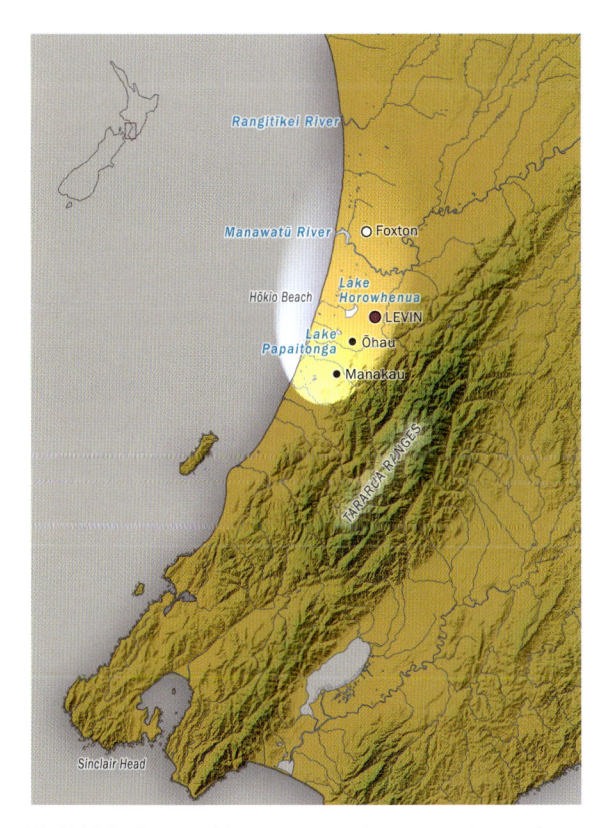

Rangitatau pā, below, at Palmer Head in Wellington, was once the residence of Ngāi Tara chief Tūteremoana. The pā was located on the prominent headland to the left in this image.

The highlighted area on this map represents the current main area of settlement of Muaūpoko people. Traditionally, they occupied an area stretching from Sinclair Head in the south to the Rangitīkei River in the north. This territory was bounded by the Tararua Ranges in the east and sea in the west.

Māori Tribes of New Zealand 79

NGĀTI RAUKAWA

> Raukawa is an aromatic plant which Māhinaarangi used as perfume for her nightly rendezvous with her Tainui lover, Tūrongo. They named their son, the ancestor of Ngāti Raukawa, after the plant. Their marriage bound together important Tainui and East Coast families and even today, some 20–25 generations later, their courtship is recounted on marae.
>
> Raukawa is both a symbol of romantic love and the head of an influential dynasty.

The ancestral home of Ngāti Raukawa is in the south Waikato and northern Taupō. Maungatautari, their mountain, is said to be divided: one side male, the other female.

The tribe's homeland became divided too. In the 19th century, some of them moved south and settled a second region stretching from Manawatū to Waikanae.

ANCESTORS

The tribe is descended from Raukawa, named after a tree with aromatic leaves. His mother had used them to perfume her skin when courting his father.

Fabled leaders include Maniapoto and Kapumanawawhiti, who carved out new territory. The great warrior chief Te Rauparaha was also of Ngāti Raukawa descent.

THE MIGRATION SOUTH

Facing endless land battles with Waikato tribes, Te Rauparaha moved south with his people, Ngāti Toarangatira. In the early 1820s he encouraged Ngāti Raukawa to migrate too. The people were unsure, but when another chief burnt down their pā, they were forced to leave.

This was the first of three migrations. On their long journeys they encountered tragedy and conflict. The leader of the third movement, Te Whatanui, achieved many successes but when invited to return north he replied, 'Should I, Ngāti Raukawa, return to Maungatautari? To the home abandoned from the heart? … I dread to be looked on as a visitor.'

Maungatautari, just south of Cambridge, is the traditional mountain of Ngāti Raukawa.

NGĀTI RAUKAWA TODAY

Many Ngāti Raukawa people moved to the cities after the Second World War. In 1975 they started a successful programme to revive their marae and the language.

The community is flourishing in both regions. Ōtaki is a centre of Ngāti Raukawa culture, with Raukawa marae, Te Rauparaha's beautifully restored Rangiātea Church, and the tribal centre of higher learning, Te Wānanga-o-Raukawa. In 2006, more than 29,000 people claimed descent from the tribe.

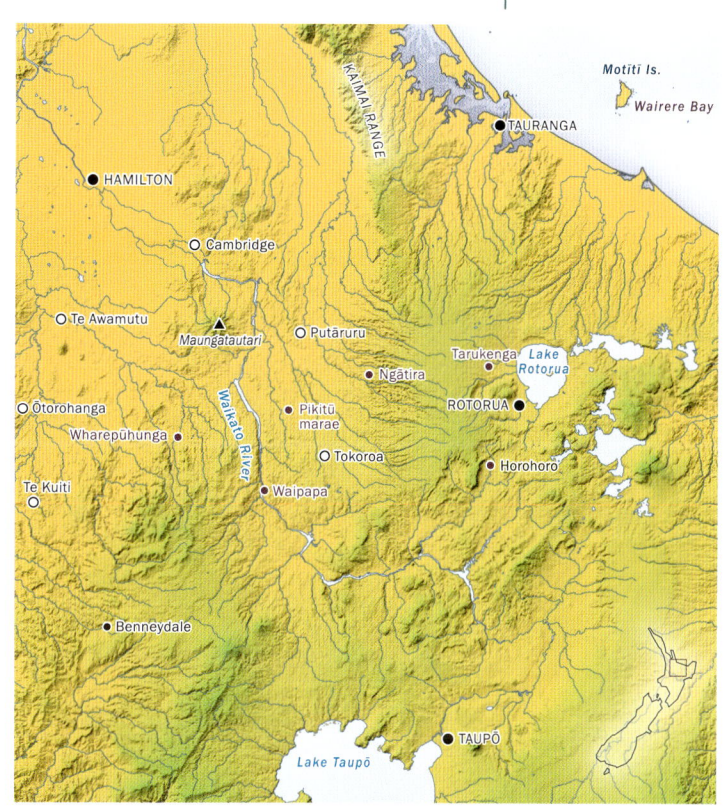

Ngāti Raukawa's ancestral home is in the southern Waikato and northern Taupō area. Their ancestral mountain is Maungatautari. One part of their homelands, called Wharepūhunga, stretches down from Te Awamutu to Waipapa. A second area, Te Kaokaoroa-o-Pātetere, goes north-east from northern Taupō towards the Kaimai Range. Their leading marae are marked in colour.

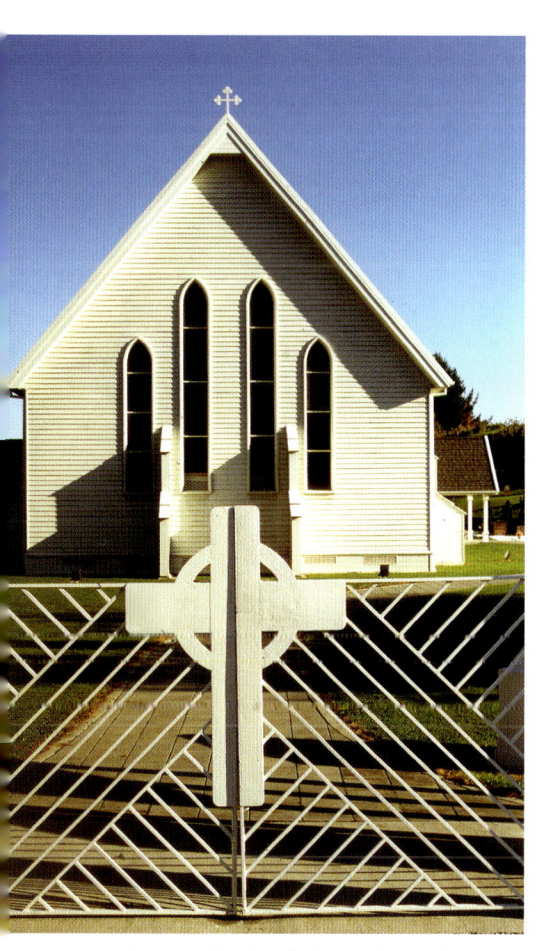

Rangiātea Church, in Ōtaki, was the shared vision of Ngāti Toa chief Te Rauparaha and early missionaries, especially Octavius Hadfield and Samuel Williams. Completed in 1851, it was one of New Zealand's finest Māori churches. In 1995 it was burnt down by an arsonist. The local people raised funds to build a replica (shown here), which opened in 2003.

Some Ngāti Raukawa migrated to Horowhenua in the early 1820s. They settled between the Rangitīkei River and the Kukutauaki Stream This district is referred to as 'Mai i Waitapu ki Rangataua mai i Mīria-te-kakara ki Kukutauaki' – meaning, 'from Waitapu to Rangataua (two steams flowing into the Rangitīkei River), and from Mīria-te-kakara (location in the Rangitīkei River) to Kukutauaki'.

Māori Tribes of New Zealand 81

NGĀTI TOARANGATIRA

The Ngāti Toarangatira people, originally from Kāwhia, have survived changing fortunes. Led by the famous warrior chief Te Rauparaha, they walked south in search of a safer and more prosperous life.

After facing hardships along the way, they became a rich and powerful tribe on both sides of Cook Strait (Te Moana-a-Raukawa).

Today Ngāti Toarangatira's lands are largely in the south-western North Island, centred around Porirua and the Kapiti coast.

Ngāti Toarangatira (also known as Ngāti Toa) trace their origins to the *Tainui* canoe, captained by Hoturoa. One of Hoturoa's descendants was the chief Tūpāhau. On a famous occasion, Tūpāhau spared the life of an enemy he had defeated. After that, his people were named Toarangatira – the tribe of chivalrous and chiefly warriors. Tūpāhau's grandson, a great warrior, was also named Toarangatira.

Kapiti Island, top, is renowned as the stronghold of the Ngāti Toa tribe during the 1820s and 1830s, when the great chief Te Rauparaha made it the centre of an extensive empire.

At left is the logo of Te Rūnanga o Toa Rangatira, the Ngāti Toa tribal authority. It depicts the ancestor, Toarangatira, famed for his strong leadership qualities, military prowess and chivalry.

82   Māori Tribes of New Zealand

MIGRATION SOUTH

Ngāti Toa originally lived in the Kāwhia area on the North Island's west coast. Because of conflicts with Waikato tribes, they decided to move south to the Kapiti coast in the early 1820s. Along the way a group of them, mainly women, met a war party. Te Rauparaha, Ngāti Toa's great leader, told them to dress as chiefs and stand beside several fires, to make the enemy think there were more of them. This part of their journey became known as Te Heke Tahutahuahi (the fire-lighting migration). When they reached Taranaki they rested for several months.

They were joined by Taranaki tribes on the next part of the migration. This journey was called Te Heke Tātaramoa (the bramble bush migration), because of the many obstacles they faced. The entire migration was called Te Heke Mai-i-raro (the migration from the north).

One of Te Rauparaha's distinguishing features was his incomplete moko (facial tattoo). This close-up of the design shows a section missing at the bottom right.

THE RISE AND FALL OF NGĀTI TOA

Between 1820 and the 1840s, with Te Rauparaha as their chief, Ngāti Toa became the dominant tribe on the Kapiti coast. They also conquered territory in the South Island, and controlled large areas on both sides of Cook Strait from their island fortress of Kapiti. But after European settlers arrived, they were seen as a threat. The government kidnapped Te Rauparaha and held him prisoner. Ngāti Toa were forced to sell most of their land.

NGĀTI TOA TODAY

The representative body of Ngāti Toa, Te Rūnanga o Toa Rangatira, looks after the land, resources and mana of the tribe. It is seeking compensation for the unjust actions of the government in the past. In 2006, almost 3,500 people claimed descent from Ngāti Toa.

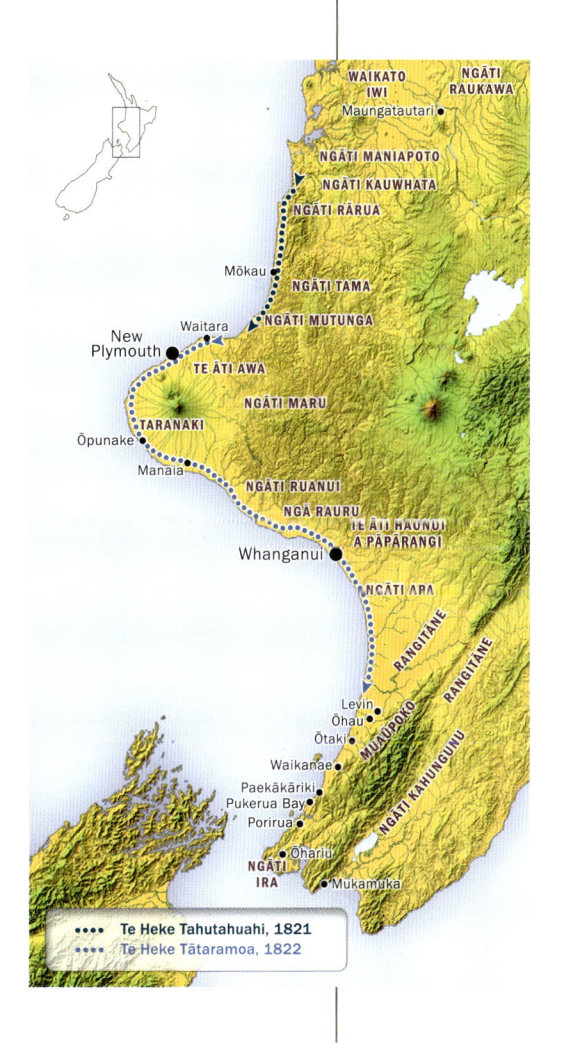

This map shows the route taken by Ngāti Toa in their journey south to the Kapiti coast and the Wellington region in the 1820s. The first part of the journey, to Taranaki, was called Te Heke Tahutahuahi (the fire-lighting migration). The second part, from Taranaki to Wellington, was called Te Heke Tātaramoa (the bramble bush migration). The entire journey was called Te Heke Mai-i-raro (the migration from the north).

Te Heke Tahutahuahi, 1821
Te Heke Tātaramoa, 1822

Māori Tribes of New Zealand

TE ĀTI AWA OF WELLINGTON

During the 1820s and 1830s, members of Te Āti Awa and other tribes left their ancestral home in Taranaki and travelled south in four great migrations, finally reaching the Kapiti coast and Wellington Harbour. After the arrival of the first English settlers in the area, many important sites were lost in the pressure for land.

The Te Āti Awa people who settled in the area of Te Whanganui-a-Tara (Wellington Harbour) are closely connected to two other tribes: Te Āti Awa of Taranaki and Ngāti Awa of the Bay of Plenty and the far north. All three are descended from Awanuiarangi, whose mother was Rongoueroa. Tradition says that Awanuiarangi's father was a spirit, Tamarau.

Rongoueroa was also the mother of Whātonga, whose father was Ruarangi. Ruarangi's father was the Polynesian explorer Toi. Whātonga's son Tara is remembered in the place name Te Whanganui-a-Tara (the great harbour of Tara).

TARANAKI ORIGINS

Between the 1820s and 1835, people of the Te Āti Awa tribe migrated to the Wellington region from Taranaki. They were forced to move south because of raids by northern tribes, particularly the Waikato people. The Ngāti Toa people were also pushed out of Kāwhia by the Waikato tribes.

Te Āti Awa moved south to Wellington in four migrations, or heke:
- Te Heke Tātaramoa, about 1822
- Te Heke Nihoputa, about 1824
- Te Heke Tamateuaua, in 1832
- Te Heke Paukena, in 1834.

This mere pounamu is called Horokiwi and is a taonga of Te Āti Awa of Wellington. One of its owners was the 19th-century chief Te Rīrā Pōrutu, who lived at Pipitea pā in Thorndon, Wellington. It is now on long-term loan to Te Papa Tongarewa, the national museum.

OTHER TRIBES IN WELLINGTON

Te Āti Awa were not the only Taranaki tribe to move south. The people of Ngāti Mutunga and Ngāti Tama also settled the Kapiti coast and Wellington region.

In 1835, when Ngāti Mutunga and some Ngāti Tama migrated to the Chatham Islands, their land around the harbour was given to Te Āti Awa and other Taranaki chiefs.

In 1839 land in the Wellington area was bought by Europeans, a town was planned, and settlers began to arrive in 1840. As a result, Māori were forced to move outside the town.

Many returned to Taranaki, but after the First World War they started moving back to Wellington to find work.

In 1835 on Matiu (Somes Island), Ngāti Mutunga transferred their rights to land around the harbour to Te Āti Awa and other Taranaki chiefs.

TE ĀTI AWA OF WELLINGTON TODAY

In 1977 the Wellington Tenths Trust was established. It represents the descendants of Te Āti Awa and other Taranaki people who lived in the Wellington area before European settlement. The trust administers the lands given to Māori in the purchase of Wellington.

In the 2006 census, more than 1,700 people said they were descended from Te Āti Awa of Wellington.

The Wellington Tenths

In 1839 the New Zealand Company purchased land around Wellington Harbour from some of the Māori who had customary rights there. The purchase deed provided for one-tenth of the land purchased to be reserved for the signatory chiefs and their families. This provision gave rise to the expression 'tenths', to refer to the land reserved for Māori in and around Wellington.

•••• Te Heke Tātaramoa, 1822
•••• Te Heke Nihoputa, 1824

This map shows the routes taken by Te Āti Awa and their allies during two major migrations of the 1820s, prompted by pressure in the north from aggressive Waikato tribes. In the Tātaramoa migration of about 1822, Te Āti Awa were accompanied by people of Ngāti Toa, Ngāti Mutunga and Ngāti Tama. The last two tribes also joined them on the Nihoputa migration of about 1824. Both journeys were difficult and dangerous, passing through or near the territories of many other tribes.

In 1980, at a traditional dawn ceremony, the new Pipitea marae, left, was opened. Built just below the old Pipitea pā, it was designed to cater for the growing Māori population in Wellington. Although Te Āti Awa protocol is observed on the marae, it also caters for other tribes living in Wellington.

Māori Tribes of New Zealand   85

TE TAU IHU TRIBES

Te Tau Ihu o Te Waka-a-Māui is the prow of the demigod Māui's canoe – the top of the South Island. Many different iwi (tribes) have migrated to these fertile, mineral-rich lands: the elusive 'fairy folk' of ancient times; the descendants of the navigator Kupe; and powerful Ngāti Tūmatakōkiri, who ruled for 200 years. Today, eight tribes form the region's tangata whenua population.

There are now eight tribes in Te Tau Ihu (Nelson–Marlborough):
- Ngāti Kuia, Rangitāne and Ngāti Apa (from the *Kurahaupō* canoe)
- Ngāti Koata, Ngāti Rārua and Ngāti Toa (from the *Tainui* canoe)
- Ngāti Tama and Te Āti Awa (from Taranaki).

EARLY HISTORY

Home to many tribes over the centuries, Te Tau Ihu (the top of the South Island) was rich in minerals such as argillite, prized for weapons and tools. The legend of Kaiwhakaruaki, the man-eating monster, may have kept people from stealing these treasures, and protected important routes to greenstone resources further south.

The early tribe Waitaha claimed descent from Rākaihautū, who had shaped the South Island's mountains with his magic digging stick. Waitaha were gardeners, and enriched the soil which is still fertile today. Later, Ngāti Māmoe from the north, impressed by gifts of preserved eels and birds from Nelson, pushed out Waitaha and seized the resources for themselves.

The Polynesian ancestor Kupe named many places, including Te Taero-a-Kereopa, the Boulder Bank which forms Nelson Harbour. When chasing Kereopa, who had kidnapped his daughter, Kupe was held back by this barrier of rocks falling from a bluff.

The ancestors of Ngāti Kuia, a long-established Nelson tribe, arrived from Hawaiki on the *Kurahaupō* canoe. During the 16th and 17th centuries, Ngāti Tūmatakōkiri and other North Island tribes moved into the region.

Ngāti Kuia first settled in the Pelorus area and then spread out across the Marlborough Sounds, Nelson and Tasman districts to Taitapu on the West Coast, and as far south as the Nelson lakes. This view looking west over Pelorus Sound is from Parorangi (Mt Stokes), the highest point in the Sounds and a place of considerable significance to the tribe.

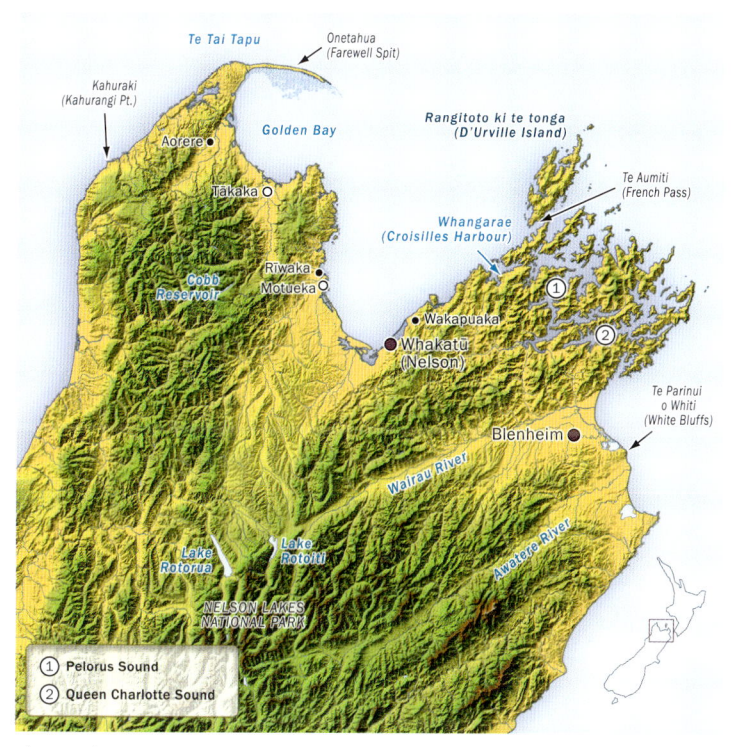

This map shows places of significance to the tribes of Te Tau Ihu both today and in the past.

EUROPEAN CONTACT

Māori encountered Europeans for the very first time in 1642, when the Dutch explorer Abel Tasman arrived at present-day Golden Bay. It ended in bloodshed: the Ngāti Tūmatakōkiri people killed four of his crew members. But when Captain James Cook arrived in the 1770s, relations were mostly friendly – Cook stayed for over six months in Queen Charlotte Sound.

In the 1820s tribes from Kāwhia and Taranaki, led by the great warrior Te Rauparaha, conquered the region and began farming, building, and trading with whalers.

From 1842 European settlers arrived. At first they got on well with Māori, and trade flourished, but questionable purchases of land caused trouble. Māori continued to lose ownership of their land for over 100 years, and tribal ways of life suffered.

TE TAU IHU TRIBES TODAY

The Wakatū Incorporation was established in 1977. It has regained lands and started fishing, forestry and other ventures. They run many community projects, including marae restoration and health centres. In 2006, more than 8,200 people claimed affiliation with the Te Tau Ihu tribes.

This carving stands in the Wakatū Incorporation's registered office in Nelson. The Wakatū Incorporation, established in 1977, oversees the assets and lands of the Nelson Tenths. The circular top of the carving incorporates Wakatū's logo, showing a koru (fern frond), rising up as a wave, with a symbolic canoe prow. The base represents the history of the Nelson area. The central figure at the bottom is Te Rauparaha and the small figures down each side represent the original chiefs of the four tribes, Ngāti Koata, Ngāti Rarua, Ngāti Tama and Te Āti Awa, who were the original owners of the Nelson Native Reserve lands now vested in the Wakatū Incorporation.

Māori Tribes of New Zealand

NGĀI TAHU

Migrating from the North Island's East Coast, Ngāi Tahu thrived in the South Island. They intermarried with local tribes, and adopted their beliefs. Their lands cover much of Te Wai Pounamu – the South Island – and are New Zealand's largest single tribal territory.

Ngāi Tahu trace their tribal identity back to Paikea, who lived in the Polynesian homeland of Hawaiki. To escape being killed at sea by his brother, he came to New Zealand on the back of a whale. Ngāi Tahu share this ancestor with the Ngāti Porou people. One of Paikea's descendants was Tahupōtiki, from whom Ngāi Tahu take their name. He lived on the East Coast of the North Island.

From the East Coast, Ngāi Tahu migrated south, first to Wellington, then across Cook Strait to the South Island. This was known as Te Wai Pounamu, the greenstone waters – named after the beautiful and valuable stone found on the West Coast. As Ngāi Tahu moved down the island they fought several battles with two tribes already living there: Ngāti Māmoe and Waitaha. By the end of the 18th century Ngāi Tahu had reached Foveaux Strait at the bottom of the South Island, and occupied the West Coast.

THE LAND

It was not just through warfare that Ngāi Tahu came to occupy much of the South Island. They also mixed with Ngāti Māmoe and Waitaha through marriages with the families of chiefs. They studied and adopted the traditions and history of Waitaha, whose ancestor Rākaihautū is said to have carved out the South Island's lakes and mountains with his digging stick. Waitaha believed the landmarks surrounding them were their ancestors, and that the winds were related to each other like members of a family.

Strategic marriages between Ngāi Tahu and Ngāti Mamoe helped cement the tribes together. After their marriage, Tūteurutira of Ngāi Tahu and Hinerongo of Ngāti Māmoe settled at Matariki pā, at the mouth of the Clarence River. There are several archaeological sites at the river mouth.

WARS WITH NGĀTI TOA

In the 1820s and 1830s the powerful chief Te Rauparaha led the North Island tribe Ngāti Toarangatira in attacks on Ngāi Tahu. Armed with muskets, they were seeking revenge for tribal insults and killings. They also wanted to take control of the valuable greenstone in the region. Ngāi Tahu suffered greatly. They survived for three months when Te Rauparaha surrounded their pā at Kaiapoi, but when strong winds caused a fire, the enemy rushed in and killed the people. However, Ngāi Tahu did not lose their territory. On one occasion Ngāi Tahu nearly captured Te Rauparaha himself in a surprise attack from behind a hill at Kāpara-te-hau (Lake Grassmere).

NGĀI TAHU TODAY

Ngāi Tahu sold most of their land to the British Crown between 1844 and 1863. The Crown had promised to leave some of the land and the food-gathering places in the hands of the tribe, and to provide schools and hospitals. But the government did not keep these promises, and for 150 years, Ngāi Tahu pursued a claim for compensation.

Their claim was finally settled in the 1990s. Among other things, it returned the sacred mountain of Aoraki/Mt Cook to the tribe and acknowledged their ownership of pounamu (greenstone).

In the 2006 census, almost 50,000 people said they were of Ngāi Tahu descent.

This magnificent greenstone hei tiki, above, was found at Kaiapoi pā. The pā, at the eastern end of routes across the Southern Alps, became the centre of working and trading in the prized stone pounamu (greenstone, or New Zealand jade). The stone was carried from the Arahura River in Westland across what is now Harper Pass to Kaiapoi, and from there it was traded throughout New Zealand.

This carved figure, below, sits at the top of a monument on the site of Kaiapoi pā. The monument was erected in 1898, largely on the initiative of the missionary James Stack, who was based in the nearby Ngāi Tahu village of Tuahiwi. The tall column rises from a bank reconstructed on the pā's original defences.

The Ngāi Tahu tribal area, left, embraces all of the South Island except for its northern tips. Te Parinui-o-whiti in the east and Kahurangi in the west mark the tribe's northern boundaries. By the early 19th century, Ngāi Tahu settlements were found along the east coast from Kaikōura to Foveaux Strait. Trails penetrated inland to the sites of summer food-gathering camps, and across the alps to settlements where greenstone was found.

Māori Tribes of New Zealand

MORIORI

Hundreds of years ago the Moriori, of the Chatham Islands, took a solemn vow of peace known as Nunuku's Law. The decision to uphold this sacred law in the face of aggression in 1835 had tragic consequences.
They were slaughtered, enslaved, and dispossessed of their lands. Nevertheless, the Moriori people survived.

The Moriori lived on Rēkohu (Chatham Island) and Rangiaotea (Pitt Island) – two islands in the Chatham Islands group, about 700 kilometres south-east of Wellington.

In Moriori tradition, their ancestors included people of the Wheteina and Rauru tribes of Hawaiki, who came to Rēkohu by canoe. They intermarried with people already living at Rēkohu. These people were the Hamata tribe, descended from the founding ancestor, Rongomaiwhenua.

In the 19th century this figure of the Moriori god Hatitimatangi was found in a cave. The holes in the chin may have been drilled for the attachment of a beard. It is the only example of Moriori wood sculpture known to have survived.

NUNUKU'S LAW

Isolated from mainland New Zealand, Moriori developed a unique culture based on a law of peace. This was called Nunuku's Law, after the ancestor Nunuku-whenua. After seeing bloody conflict between the Hamata people and later arrivals, he banned murder and the eating of human flesh forever.

Moriori ancestors made carved images on the trunks of kopi (karaka) trees. Many of these carvings, or dendroglyphs, survive today. They have powerful spiritual associations, although their meanings are debated.

LATER ARRIVALS

After 1791, when the British ship *Chatham* called at Rēkohu, Moriori came into contact with Europeans and Māori who came as crew on sealing and whaling vessels. Some settled on the islands and lived alongside the Moriori. This relative peace was shattered in 1835 when Māori of the Ngāti Mutunga and Ngāti Tama tribes, both from Taranaki, arrived in the Chatham Islands in search of new territories and resources.

Ngāti Mutunga and Ngāti Tama immediately began killing and enslaving the Moriori people. Although Moriori outnumbered them almost two to one, they chose to obey Nunuku's Law and did not fight back. Approximately 300 were killed, and the rest were enslaved. The tribe was in danger

This waka kōrari (wash-through raft) had a special construction to stop it capsizing in rough seas. Its base of inflated kelp and sides of bound reeds became partially submerged, giving the craft added stability.

of being destroyed completely. Following several Moriori petitions, the New Zealand government finally stepped in after 28 years. However, a land court in 1870 decided to give most of the Chatham Islands to Ngāti Tama and Ngāti Mutunga, despite the fact that most Māori had by this time returned to their homes in Taranaki.

THE MORIORI TODAY

It was once thought that Moriori were a Melanesian people. Many believed that Tommy Solomon, who died in 1933, was the last Moriori simply because he was the last known Moriori of full blood. In the 1980s it began to be accepted that Moriori shared the same Polynesian ancestry as Māori, and had living descendants. In the 1990s, Moriori began to rebuild their culture and identity. As a result of their claim to the Waitangi Tribunal, the Moriori were recognised as the indigenous people of the Chatham Islands.

Chatham Island Moriori are active in conservation, commercial fisheries, tourism and other ventures. The Moriori language is gradually being revived. In January 2005 Moriori celebrated the opening of their marae and cultural centre, Te Kopinga (meaning 'kopi grove'). In the 2006 census, 945 people said they were of Moriori descent.

These planks are from the front of a Moriori house that is thought to have been standing at Ōwenga in the 1840s. They are the only surviving examples of Moriori construction.

The oldest Moriori artefacts have been uncovered on the shoreline of Pitt Island. In the background rises the ancient remnant volcano Hakepa, also the highest point on the island.

URBAN MĀORI

The movement of Māori from their traditional homelands to the cities was among the fastest of any population.

In 1926, 84% were living in rural, tribal settlements. By 1986, just under 80% were in urban centres.

Such a dramatic displacement into a strange new world led to isolation and a sense of loss. But with the revival of their language and culture from the 1970s, urban Māori have forged a new and vibrant pan-tribal identity.

MOVING TO THE CITIES

Before the Second World War, most Māori lived with other members of their tribes in rural areas. During the 1940s, many young Māori not eligible for military service worked in industries in the cities. From the 1950s, there was a growing demand for labour in the cities, and by 2006 almost 85% of Māori were living in towns or cities.

Most headed to the cities in search of work, but they were also hoping for money, fun and adventure. Initially some Pākehā resisted the migration of Māori, but over time, friendships developed and intermarriage increased. The government encouraged Māori to leave rural areas, and to adapt to European society. By the 1960s, there was a generation of young Māori who had been born in the cities. Many did not know about their tribal roots.

When Noel Hilliard's Maori girl *was published in 1960 it sparked controversy because it depicted the racial discrimination encountered by a young Māori woman who moves from a small rural community to Wellington.*

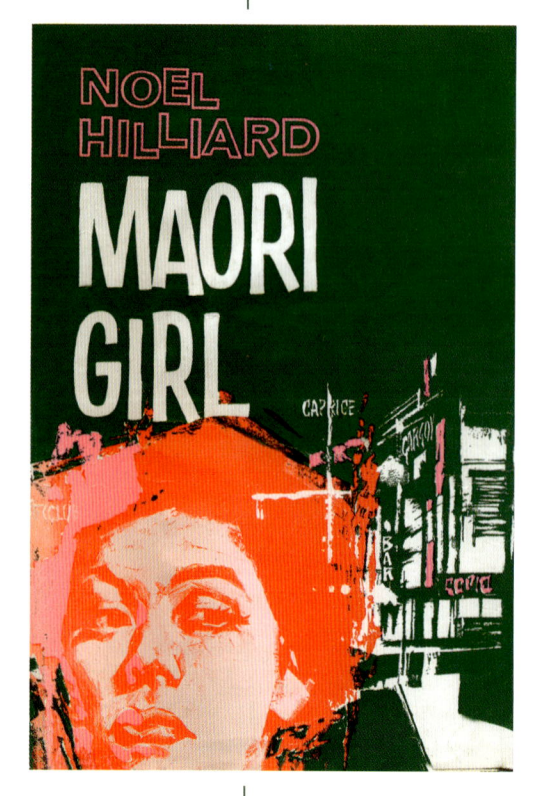

CHALLENGES

Towns and cities offered better paid work and more opportunities, which many Māori enjoyed. But there were also difficulties. The first arrivals mainly found unskilled manual work, which was vulnerable in times of economic downturn.

Māori often faced discrimination when looking for a place to live, so hostels and state housing were built for them. Māori communities developed in some suburbs, such as Porirua and Ōtara. But some Māori found it difficult to cope living far from their home communities, without the support of their extended family. Often they became lonely, had money troubles, or drifted into crime.

Being cut off from traditional ways of life meant that the children of these migrants often lacked a sense of Māori identity.

Members of an Auckland-based Ngāi Tūhoe group, Te Tira Hōu, perform at Te Hui Ahurei at Rūātoki in 2003. This festival is held every two years by the Tūhoe tribe, drawing many urban members back to the tribal area to renew their ties and enjoy cultural and sporting activities.

GROUP SUPPORT

Māori in the cities banded together to form clubs, social committees and cultural groups, such as the Ngāti Pōneke Young Māori Club in Wellington. Some tribes formed groups to support their members in the cities, and protest groups developed from the 1970s.

Far from their home regions, people missed the marae, the place where they would gather and mark important social events such as birthdays, weddings and tangi (funerals). In the 1960s projects to build urban marae began. Now there are urban marae in major cities. They provide a place where urban Māori of different tribes feel they belong.

Since the 1980s there have been urban Māori organisations, such as Te Whānau o Waipareira Trust of West Auckland. They say that Māori living in the towns and cities are like a separate tribe, with their own interests and problems. The groups have fought for the right to manage social welfare and education programmes for their members, and to receive the benefits from Treaty of Waitangi claims. This development has challenged old ideas about the tribal basis of Māori society.

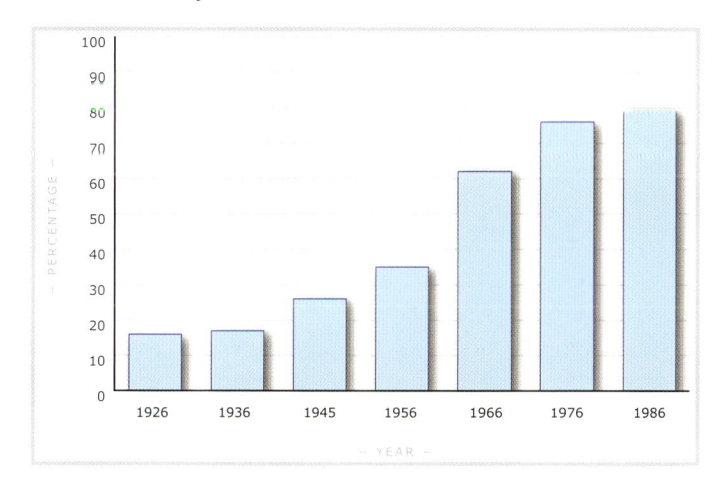

This graph shows the increase in the percentage of Māori living in urban areas between 1926 and 1986. The rate of urban migration was particularly rapid after the Second World War. Source: Ian Pool, Te Iwi Māori. Auckland: Auckland University Press, 1991, pp. 123, 154, 182, 197.

Social upheaval

Pita Sharples, one of the founders of Hoani Waititi urban marae, describes the social problems he observed among Māori who came to live in Auckland in the 1950s and 60s: 'The change from the rural to an urban way of life was a huge culture shock. So many families were soon run down and the children were in trouble. They were broke, they had their power and water cut off, they owed rates and stuff like this. The discipline of the city was totally different from the discipline of the country. So there were huge problems.'

Māori Tribes of New Zealand

GLOSSARY

haka
dance of challenge and welcome; chant accompanying a dance with actions

hapū
descent group, clan; modern meaning: section of a tribe, secondary tribe; literally: to have conceived

hui
meeting, assembly, coming together

iwi
set of people bound together by descent from a common ancestor or ancestors; literally: bone; modern meaning: tribe

kāinga
home, place of abode, lodgings, quarters

mana
authority, power, psychic force, prestige

marae
open space or courtyard where people gather, generally in front of a main building or meeting house; forum of social life; modern meaning: the complex of buildings surrounding the courtyard and the courtyard itself

mauri
life principle; material object that is a symbol of the hidden principle protecting vitality

pā
fortified refuge or settlement

Pākehā
non-Māori, usually of British ethnic origin or background

patupaiarehe
elusive 'fairy' peoples that usually lived in forests or on mountains

pounamu
New Zealand jade (nephrite or bowenite), commonly called greenstone

rangatira
well-born, well-bred person; chief, male or female; leader of a tribe

rūnanga
tribal or public assembly, conference, council

tangata whenua
literally: person or people of the land; people belonging to a tribal region; hosts as distinct from visitors

taniwha
guardian, legendary monster

tapu
sacred; under religious restriction

tohunga
priest; expert in traditional lore; person skilled in specific activity; healer

waiata
chant, song, poetry; to chant, to sing

whakapapa
genealogical table; to recite in proper order; literally: to place in layers

whānau
extended family group; to be born; modern meaning: family

whare
house, dwelling

PICTURE CREDITS

AAG	Auckland Art Gallery Toi o Tāmaki
ANZ	Archives New Zealand Te Rua Mahara o Te Kāwanatanga
ATL	Alexander Turnbull Library
AWMM	Auckland War Memorial Museum Te Paenga Hira
CM	Canterbury Museum
DB	David Bateman Ltd.
DOC	Department of Conservation
GNS	GNS Science
MONZ	Museum of New Zealand Te Papa Tongarewa
NSIL	Natural Sciences Image Library
NZH	*New Zealand Herald*
TWA	Te Wānanga o Aotearoa
TA	Te Ara – the Encyclopedia of New Zealand

Maps and diagrams are copyright to Te Ara – the Encyclopedia of New Zealand. Unless noted otherwise, credits are listed by page number, from top to bottom of the page.

7 University of Auckland, Department of Anthropology Photographic Archive; AWMM AU 1785; TA, photograph by Jock Phillips
8 MONZ
9 *NZH* 13 April 2000, photograph by Nicola Topping; MONZ F.003617/09
10 University of Waikato, photograph by David Lowe
11 ATL E-011-f-004, watercolour by William Mein Smith; DOC 1033848, photograph by Dick Veitch; DOC, photograph by Kevin Jones
12 AAG, lithograph by Antoine Maurin after Louis-Auguste de Sainson
13 AAG
14 TA, photograph by Shirley Williams
15 MONZ B.042451
16 ATL; TA, photograph by Carl Walrond
17 TA, photograph by Shirley Williams; Victoria University of Wellington, Te Herenga Waka Marae, photograph by Miranda Wells
18 Waipapa Marae, University of Auckland, photograph by Melanie Lovell-Smith
19 DOC 10050812, photograph by Chris Rudge; TA, photograph by Rangi McGarvey
20 DOC
21 Te Wānanga o Aotearoa; GNS 43896/10, photograph by Lloyd Homer
22 ATL PUBL-0014-15, tinted lithograph by J. W. Giles
23 AAG, oil painting by Gottfried Lindauer; ATL PUBL-0014-19, tinted lithograph after drawing by George French Angas
24 AWMM; DOC
25 AWMM Ethno 280
26 AWMM; ATL A-114-045, pencil and ink drawing by Thomas Kendall
27 TA, photograph by Jock Phillips; DOC, photograph by Kevin Jones
28 TA, photograph by Melanie Lovell-Smith
29 DB, photograph by Russell McGeorge; WINZ Whangarei Service Centre, carving by Te Warihi Hetaraka
30 DOC 10047681, photograph by Lisa Forester
31 NZH, photograph by Russell Smith
32 TA, photograph by Melanie Lovell-Smith
33 GNS 1897/23, photograph by Lloyd Homer; GNS 22841/18, photograph by Lloyd Homer
34 DOC 10048829
35 GNS 17584, photograph by Lloyd Homer
36 AWMM
37 DB, photograph by Russell McGeorge
38 (left) TA, photograph by Roberta McKelvey; (right) GNS 22622/23, photograph by Lloyd Homer
39 GNS 513/15, photograph by Lloyd Homer
40 TWA
41 TWA (both)
42 Rotorua Museum of Art and History, photograph by Paul Tapsell
43 DB, photograph by Russell McGeorge
44 TA, photograph by Leanne Tamaki
45 DB, photograph by Russell McGeorge
46 TA, photograph by Shirley Williams
47 TA, photograph by Shirley Williams
48 TA, photograph by Peter Hodsell
49 Te Whare Wānanga o Awanuiārangi, photograph by Lynne Raumati; TA, photograph by Jock Phillips
50 (left) TA, photograph by Shirley Williams;(right) Whakatane District Museum and Gallery
51 TA, photograph by Shirley Williams
52 GNS 9147/22, photograph by Lloyd Homer
53 Private collection, photograph by Leanne Tamaki
54 MONZ
55 (left) ATL John Dobrée Pascoe Collection (PAColl-0783) F-1090-1/4, photograph by John Dobrée Pascoe; GNS SL/101/3, photograph by Lloyd Homer
56 GNS 41063, photograph by Lloyd Homer; Te Runanga o Ngati Porou
57 TA, photograph by Jock Phillips
58 TA, photograph by Jock Phillips
59 ATL A-173-031, ink drawing by Gilbert Mair
60 TA, photograph by Leanne Tamaki
61 TA, photograph by Leanne Tamaki; TA, photograph by Shirley Williams
62 *Hawke's Bay Today* 2 December 2004, photograph by Warren Buckland
63 (left) TA, photograph by Leanne Tamaki; (right) MONZ F.002607/12
64 AWMM, carving by Wiremu Kingi Te Rangitake
65 NSIL, photograph by Harley Betts
66 TA, photograph by Jock Phillips
67 (left) Puke Ariki Taranaki Museum & Library, photograph by Christine Whybrew; (right) MONZ, acrylic on paper by Ralph Hotere
68 TA, photograph by Jock Phillips
69 TA, photograph by Jock Phillips
70 MONZ F.7056/41 W. F. Gordon, Te Ua flag
71 MONZ F.004876/12, glasswork by Darcy Nicholas; PhotoNewZealand/Paul Stieller
72 Private collection, photograph by David Young
73 MONZ
74 Te Rūnanga o Ngāti Apa
75 Bateman, photograph by Russell McGeorge
76 Bateman, photograph by Russell McGeorge
77 TA, photograph by Zoe Dewson; Tanenuiarangi Manawatu Incorporated, photograph by Zoe Dewson
78 TA, photograph by Jock Phillips
79 Muaūpoko Tribal Authority Incorporated; TA, photograph by Jock Phillips
80 TA, photograph by Shirley Williams
81 Private Collection, photograph by Chris Maclean
82 Shutterstock/Graeme Knox; Te Runanga o Toarangatira
83 ANZ NZC 133, 24 (1)
84 MONZ I.00668
85 ATL Dominion Post Collection (PAColl-7327) EP/1980/1751/19A; GNS 38754-5, photograph by Lloyd Homer
86 TA, photograph by Jock Phillips
87 Wakatū Incorporation
88 GNS 19740/21, photograph by Lloyd Homer
89 CM E163.254; TA, photograph by Jock Phillips
90 (left) MONZ I.006386, photograph by Brian Brake; Bateman, photograph by Russell McGeorge
91 MONZ F.004324/03,04,07,08; MONZ I.006386; AWMM, photograph by Robin Morrison
92 Reed Publishing New Zealand, Noel Hilliard, *Maori girl*. London: Heinemann, 1960
93 TA, photograph by Leanne Tamaki